FROM HELL TO HEAVEN

Testimony of Ashegh Masih

Ashegh Masih

ISBN-10: 0982884303
ISBN-13: 978-0-9828843-0-0

All rights reserved. This book is protected by the copyright laws of the United States of America. This book may not be copied or reprinted for commercial gain or profit.

Edited by Daniel Ibrahim.

Scripture taken from the New King James Version®. Copyright © 1982 by Thomas Nelson. Used by permission. All rights reserved.

Scripture in Farsi taken from the TPV version. All rights reserved.

"Jesus the King" used with permission.

Ashegh's testimony was also shared on the Internet and can be viewed at:
https://youtu.be/Gk68mege8II

CONTENTS

1	Born Under Oppression	Pg. 4
2	The First Miracle for Me	Pg. 14
3	Betrayal & Oppression	Pg. 20
4	I Survived Sharia Law	Pg. 28
5	Pictorial Account	Pg. 36
6	Persian Poem	Pg. 42
7	Religion of War	Pg. 44
8	Oppression of Women	Pg. 61
9	The Lord's Prayer	Pg. 74
10	The Apostles' Creed	Pg. 76
11	Universal Declaration of Human Rights	Pg. 78
12	Cyrus the Great	Pg. 96
13	Excerpts from The Gospels	Pg. 116
14	More Persian Poetry	Pg. 162
15	Jesus the King (Messiah)	Pg. 166

CHAPTER 1
BORN UNDER OPPRESSION

Greetings to my dear brothers and sisters and whoever may be listing to my words. I want to introduce myself to my friends and dear ones, sharing briefly as to who I am. But my primary goal is to testify of Jesus Christ [the Messiah], and to tell you how He, Jesus, made an unmistakable miracle take place in my life.

I am Ashegh Rassol, lover of Mohammed of yesterday, and Ashegh Masih, lover of Christ today. I was born in 1951, in the northern part of Afghanistan, in the province of Balkh, into a very poor, deprived family. My father was a nomadic shepherd.

There is a world of difference between shepherds here in the west and in Afghanistan. Although most of the people in Afghanistan are poor, deprived and oppressed, still the most deprived ones are the shepherds and the nomads. They don't even know exactly where they were born or where they will be buried. Always moving. Always moving from one place to another, from one mountain to another, from one valley to another. Despite so much hard work, on the part of both the men and women, it's difficult to make enough money to live. Typically they live on dry bread and have one set of clothes per year. But, in spite of this, they would praise God for what they did have. There were absolutely no other pleasures in life for them.

I was born in such a time and in such a family. At that time in Afghanistan, in 1951, it was chaos—with landlords, tribal leaders, mullahs (local Islamic clerics/mosque leaders), ignorance, and a king who ruled over all of us. The government was oppressive and cruel, being selfish and self-serving. The rest of the people were without hope, condemned and helpless.

When I was seven years old, I learned I had been born in a prison, and that in reality the woman who was acting as my mother was not my mother but my aunt, my father's sister. In those days, I was not very disturbed by the fact that I did not have a mother, and that I was born in a prison. However, I was hurt slightly by my father and my aunt trying to explain things away with, "the kids are just trying to mess with you." Gradually as I went to school, especially in religious school, but also in public school, I learned geography and history and what the world was all about, that there was more to the world than what I saw and understood around me.

Finally when I grew to be around 12 years old, I told my father that I then understood that there had been criminal acts and atrocities committed against us when I was born. I went to my father and told him that I needed to know about them, and I wanted to hear the full details from him and my aunt.

I needed to know, in full detail, the whole truth, because I planned to write down the whole story of my life when I got older. This would be my way of exposing the truth. I would not be able to stand up against the ruling oppressors, but someday I intended to document everything in a book. I planned to do this when I finished my schooling.

I would put down this calamity in writing—this disaster, these tragic events—and expose them to the whole world, that the world may know what takes place in this land of Islamic culture and what is done to the poor and innocent people by the ruling ones there. This is all I would be able to do to them.

My father tried to convince me not to discuss this issue, and that he didn't want to revisit his old pain and pour salt on his old wounds. However, I still insisted, and I gradually convinced him that I needed to know these facts.

And so my father consented to tell me the story on one condition: that I not respond or react violently or harshly with the mullahs, not now or ever in the future. When I asked him why not, he said, "because here in this land only the government officials and the mullahs and landlords have authority, and their law rules." He said there is no other law, and in the court of law, I would have no rights by which to be rescued. Therefore, he was worried that in the struggle for revenge, I would destroy myself. He told me these people were bloodthirsty and that the death of others meant nothing to them. In their eyes, killing me would be like killing flies or mosquitoes.

The story begins before I was born. Following the marriage of my father and mother, their firstborn child was a daughter whom they named Mahbuba. According to so many, this girl was given by God an exceptional beauty beyond measure. She gradually blossomed in that environment and location, despite the fact that she was born into a very poor family, was lacking the very basic necessities of clothing and nutritious food, that she was the daughter of a shepherd who would chase and care for sheep.

There were two mullahs who were landlords in that area. And they were always in competition with one another over who could rule over the innocent with the most oppression, cruelty, and taxation. They had complete control and rule over everything and everyone. All of the things and beautiful people belonged to them and were under their control.

By way of background, we in Afghanistan never had a central government with a centralized law extending to all of the people equally. In the history of our country there were always groups of ruling parties dominating the land.

First, there were different governmental administrations, which came and went. They were all dictator like, being self-serving and pleasure seeking, much like the infamous pharaohs of old in Egypt. Second, in the world of Islam, there were always ruling religious mullahs that controlled the people. Third, there were the landlords of a feudal system, who ruled over sections of the land and people. These controlled, ruled and oppressed the people of the land in various ways, according to their needs and wants.

The two mullahs that my father referred to were part of the ruling religious group, and they were also landlords. They both were told of the beauty of my sister. One of them was Mullah Mohamed Omar Kahn. He already had four wives and was over 50 years old, but he wanted to marry my sister. The other lived in a village a little further away. He was also very pleasure seeking and self-serving, having seven wives at the time, which meant he had seven women in his service as servants.

This is the ungentlemanly rite of men in Islam: several mothers become the slaves of the one husband. This was not part of the law of the land of Afghanistan before Islam. It was Islamic law.

The first mullah was my father's employer. He had provided a tent to live in during the winter with permission to pitch this tent on his land and to farm there also. He put a lot of pressure on my father over Mahboba, threatening to evict him from the land where he was living and farming if he did not give his daughter to him to marry. This would have forced my father to work in the snow-covered mountains where it was bitter cold. Refusing this demand would be a virtual death sentence for the whole family.

Therefore, my father had no choice but to submit to the mullah's demand. He had to drink this bitter cup and give his 14-year-old daughter, who was as beautiful as a flower, to marry a man over fifty years old who already had four other wives and several children.

Now when the other mullah who was also a landlord heard about this, he was furious, and summoned my father to his castle. There my father was treated very rudely and roughly and asked why he went against this mullah's wishes in giving the girl he wanted to his competitor? He said that because he was the first one to fall in love with her, and the first one to ask for her hand in marriage, My father had wronged him twice. "First," he said, "you denied me the woman I wanted, and second, you rewarded my competitor of what was to come to me!" Therefore, this mullah-landlord had my father put into his private prison.
He told my father that he would remain in prison till he was willing to go get his daughter from the other mullah, make the other mullah divorce her, and bring her to him for marriage. Only then he could be freed.

When my real mother was informed of what had been done to my father, knowing in that land she had no right to complain and ask for justice, she went to the ruling mullah who had put her husband in prison to intercede. At that time, my mother was pregnant with me. She went to the mullah, crying and begging him to release her husband, since he was the provider of the family and they were so poor, and that without her husband's work, they would probably starve to death.

She explained that they were employed by the other mullah-landlord and had no choice but to obey him, that they were forced to do so in order to keep their job and livelihood. She went on to explain, "If we had disobeyed him and given the girl to you, then he would have taken the tent and the land from us and we would be destitute. You are both so powerful and we are nothing in comparison, so that either way we are condemned." She begged him to please, have mercy and kindness and release her husband. But no matter how much she begged and cried, the mullah did not listen and was not willing to release her husband.

Therefore, my mother, in order to try and save her husband said, "If you are not going to release my husband, then let me be in prison with him. If you are going to kill him, then you might as well kill me also. There is no other option for me, since I will certainly die of starvation without my husband." She said these things in hope that this hard-hearted mullah landlord would feel sorry for her and have compassion on her husband. But, the mullah's answer was, "No! He ruined my pride and destroyed my glory among the people, therefore. I will get my revenge from the other mullah-landlord by putting you through this."

Now this mullah was not an ordinary Muslim. He had gone to Mecca on the pilgrimage and was well versed in the Koran and the Hadith. He knew all about Allah and. He knew almost everything Islamic. He was still willing to act in this ungodly way.

So the Mullah landlord said, "OK, if that is the way you want it, you can go to prison with your husband." So they put her in confinement with my father. I do not know where it was, a barn, stable or a dungeon.

Because of all the pressure and stress and tension on my mother, she went into labor before the natural due date. One night, at around eight to eight and a half months of pregnancy she went into labor. She and my father were alone there. No matter how much they pounded on the door, there was no answer. The door was locked and all were asleep in the place next door.

So my mother gave birth to me in the middle of the night in that locked prison. The only thing she asked after the delivery was if it was a boy or a girl. My father said, "Praise Allah, it is a boy." She smiled and while tears were coming down her cheeks, she entered into eternity. So this is how I was born, and my father gave me the name Ashegh Rasool meaning, "the lover of Mohammad."

The next morning the guards came and found my father and he explained to them what had happened the night before, how he lost his wife while she gave early birth to me in those conditions. And this real Muslim and true follower of Islam, a proud and tyrannical avenger, ordered us to be released.

So that we could bury our dead, he even assigned a peer, another mullah, to perform the burial ceremony according to Islamic laws and rituals.

My father transferred the responsibility of my care his sister, Rhobia, and she accepted me as her own child. She raised me on goat's milk, even though she herself was very poor. She tried her best and used every possible means to keep me alive and care for me. I was fed goat's milk. Unfortunately, my lips never tasted my mother's milk. My aunt raised me until I was seven years old and ready to go to school.

They wanted me to go to both a religious school and the public one. I was very excited and happy to go to both schools. I was learning the religious teachings as well as the other courses, and I was feeling very lucky to be going to school. However with the passing of time, I slowly realized these childhood feelings were untrue and unwarranted. I gradually realized that I was really not very fortunate.

I came to understand this through suffering and persecution from the Islamic world. I saw how unfortunate I really was and what a good life is supposed to be. I understood this most clearly when I became a Christian, when Jesus Christ gave me spiritual salvation and eternal life.

Several years after my real mother died, Rhobia died also. Meanwhile, my sister whose only crime in life was her God-given beauty, could not tolerate the pressures of life and died at the age of 16. The pressure of watching the cruel oppression of her mother and father and myself, on account of her, was more than she could bear.

CHAPTER 2
THE FIRST MIRACLE FOR ME

While I was undergoing my religious study in Pakistan, I studied commentaries of the Koran and the Hadith and read the writings of different Islamic writers. Eventually, I went to Iran for my higher education and studied at the University of Tehran. I was doing research in the religious, political and educational fields, as well as in other areas.

It was in those days that I learned that, whereas in Afghanistan and Pakistan, the Muslims are mostly Sunnis, by contrast in Iran the dominate belief system was Shiite. And these two sects of Islam were as different as night and day. On occasion, this question would arouse in my mind: why were there difference between the two groups? Why do the Iranians believe in Ali and his decedents as Imams? Ali was the son-in-law of Mohammed and considered the first and only caliph. While in contrast the Sunni's believe in four caliphs. I was puzzled over these differences and about who was right?

I chose a major in education and journalism at the University of Tehran, thinking to myself that educating people is the best way of freeing them from the bondage of ignorance that they remained chained to under rulers and oppressive governments. This was the one way I figured I could serve the people: to let them know about today's pharaohs.

For this reason, I spent almost 25 years, in a most remote area of Afghanistan teaching, educating, encouraging and persuading people of their rights, for example, the rights of a mother. I was there till around 1995, educating them that they would know they are human beings with certain God-given rights in society. I was doing my best to defend the rights of the poor women of Afghanistan who had been so oppressed in our culture.

Many of these women had been treated like slaves by men. Often, several women in one household had served the desires of one selfish, pleasure-seeking, ignorant man who called himself, "husband." They were being used as property and personal belongings. The Koran refers to a woman as a "Keshtzar," meaning, "a farmland," — a very insulting term for a women (it actually relates to sexual use & abuse). We will discuss this more in chapter 8.

We in Afghanistan have experienced, many times, the power of the colonizer who occupied our land. They came and went. We must be careful not to simply replace one dangerous colonizer with another. Much blood is being shed in vain.

We see now in history how, when the Russian occupiers finally left in 1989, after millions of lives were lost ridding us of these Russian criminals, the government was then replaced by the power of Islamic occupiers. This shocked even the regular

Muslims of the country. These occupiers created a fear that was worse than before!

When the criminal Mujahidin entered Kabul of Afghanistan, in 1992, they did things to people that had never been seen in the sea of humanity. After the Mujahidin, in 1996 a branch called the Taliban, related to the Al Qaeda group, took over. They were supposedly the true, devout Muslims and Islamic worshipers. They entered Afghanistan and eventually occupied a big portion of the country.

Before the Mujahidin and the Taliban took over, I had been a teacher at a girl's school. In the final days before the Taliban took over, in 1996, I was involved in education and also started a library and bookstore. This was both my way of making a living and illuminating people. I wanted to help them to be open-minded and aware of other things. I was trying to teach to people their rights as a human being and as a citizen. I always considered the freedom and God given rights of all human beings.

I lost my job as a girl's schoolteacher when the school was closed and the girls were driven to the corner of their houses in fear. They feared for their lives because of war, and they feared being beaten and raped. So at this point, I needed a new job for income. I also wanted to continue my goal of changing my world, by informing people of their rights and educating them.

I believed that if there is going to be a change in the country, it had to be a fundamental change, a change from the system of rulership by Islamic religious clerics, a change of the culture and occupying force which had been put on us 1400 years before by Islam. I still had Islamic faith, more or less, and had absolutely no contact with the Christian world at that time, neither within our country nor outside. I never had access to a Bible, and never read it or studied it. The only thing I knew about Christianity was what I was told in the Koran and from Islam.

At one point, I went from Kabul to another city of Afghanistan called Herat, a border city to the Iranian border and business center. In that city, there was a businessman who imported books and reading material from Iran for distribution throughout the country. I had done business with this person before, and I purchased 6000 copies of a variety of books in a bundle from this wholesaler who got them from Mashhad and other big cities of Iran. They were all bundled together and packed together in big crates. I brought all of these books to Kabul, to a bookstore I had started, in the center of the city. The name of this bookstore was "Aria."

I ended up putting the books away, realizing that these foolish Mujahidin, these enemies of science and education and knowledge, not only dislike books themselves, but also are against books. They are enemies of books, education, science, and civilization. Furthermore, at that time the atmosphere of the city had become so dark and gloomy that people were only concerned with how to keep from starving or how to escape, to save themselves and their family from terror and ignorance.

Therefore my bookstore was at a standstill, and my financial state was worsening. Because Kabul was constantly under fire from bombs, mortars and rockets, I moved everything to my personal home on the outskirts of Kabul to save my valuable books and myself. I put them all in the house.

Kabul was like a jungle, full of people killing each other like wild animals. It was very chaotic with many factions, foreign and domestic, Sunni and Sikh, Arab and Pakistani fighting each other. It was a very unsafe environment for families. So out of concern for my wife and the children, I managed to send them out to Pakistan to a friend's house. But I stayed behind to protect our house and the household items we had gathered over the years. I just could not leave it all behind and flee the country. So I accepted the fact that it could mean my death, and I figured, if it is to be, so be it.

I had spent close to fifty years of my life accumulating the house and what was in it and was not willing to throw it all away to save my life. Some of the 6000 books I had purchased from Iran were still in the packages and bundles. When I started opening some of the boxes to organize and put them on the shelves in our house, mixed in among them was a copy of the Holy Bible in the Farsi language. Do you see how this miracle is being formed here, and how God is working a miracle, to perform His purposes in my Life? How this Bible appeared suddenly and miraculously?

Please note that this happened even though the Bible

is forbidden for purchase and sale in Iran and is illegal. The Christians that live in Iran also must live in the hell created by Islam. They live in a hell created by the wicked Khomeini. Also in Afghanistan, the books of any religion, especially the Bible of the Christians, were absolutely forbidden. There is a penalty for owning one. No one can own, read or study this book. This was completely illegal and forbidden by the government. No Muslim can bring one into the country or is allowed to read it.

In Afghanistan 98% of the people are Muslims. 1% of the people are Hindus and Sikhs; they live there in the worst possible conditions as if they are in the hell of Islam. Other minorities make up the other 1% of the country. Of the Muslims, about 18% are Shiite and about 80% are Sunnis. Therefore, the only way for a Bible to be brought into Afghanistan was through the foreigners for their personal use, whether diplomats, Christians or Jews working at the consulates and embassies, or others. They were only permitted to use them in the privacy of their homes and for their own study and religious activities. There was absolutely no permission for the Muslims or Muslim born persons to have or read a Bible.

Now you see what a miracle it was when God put this Bible into my hands mixed in with 6000 other books. In this way, for the first time in my life, I came into to possession of a Bible! At first I was wondering to myself if an enemy had planted it there as a way to defame or get me into trouble. This was my first reaction. But as I researched the situation, I realize this was a complete accident. An exceptional incident!

I concluded that no one could have plotted to put this in the box to attack me, so here, for the first time, I came to see a Bible. And I started to read it and to study it. I really enjoyed studying this Bible. We were never allowed to have one, to read it or study it.

Even though the Gospels and the Torah are mentioned in the Koran as the books of God, they are never read or studied. I remember once before talking to an Islamic clergyman. I told him that according to Islam, when a person believes in God he needs to believe a few important things. For in Islam, it is said, we should believe in Allah and the books, meaning the books before Islam: the Torah (the "Old Testment of the Bible"), the Injil ("the Gospels"), the Zabur ("the Psalms"), the Prophets (which includes the ancient prophets of the Bible), and also in the Day of Resurrection ("the Book of Revelation"). How can we believe in a book that we are not permitted to read?

It is the same with the Torah. How can I believe in the Torah if I have never seen it and don't know what it says? How could I believe in Jesus or Moses when you have abolished them? You say believe and then you say that they have been canceled out and their words abrogated.

CHAPTER 3
BETRAYAL & OPPRESSION

I started reading the Bible. When I read it, I said to myself over and over, "Woe unto us that we have not been able to read this book before! Why have we never had the opportunity to get it and read it and study it and learn from it? This book is all about love and kindness!"

I've used an expression, "from hell to heaven," to refer to going from the world of Islam to the world of Christianity. The world of Christianity is full of love and kindness. There is no enmity or revenge, nor killing nor Jihad. And there is not the cutting off of the hands and feet of your enemy. How do you define love? God says, "I am the God of love," and, "If your enemy does you harm, pray blessing on him. Forgive your enemy. If your enemy hits you on the face, turn also the other cheek to him."

Now I compared, and I saw that the Koran, the book of Islam, is a man-made book that teaches hatred and making enemies. Human beings are an enemy. Women are an enemy. Freedom is an enemy. Life is an enemy. It is basically anti-human. It is anti-being and anti-science. It is anti and against everything that is good and created by God. There is no freedom in this book. There is no freedom of thought. All of the freedom and rights that God has granted to people are taken away.

According to the Koran, we are not to talk about love and kindness. We are told that we need to kill the Jews and the Christians. We need to kill the kafir ("infidel" or "sinner") when he denies Allah, also the moshriq (one who believes in many gods). We are told that we need to stay forever with the religion of Islam that was forced on us 1400 years ago and that we have no right to change. There is no greater oppression in the history of mankind than this.

So I studied the Bible that I got. However, the issue of being baptized or having any kind of outside relationship anywhere in the world, as I was later accused of, was absolutely a lie and never took place. I say that now, even when there is absolutely no danger of being persecuted by them keeping me from telling the truth. There is absolutely no fear of physical harm to make me lie to you out of fear. Thankfully, I have victory over fear and victory over death. I have been saved.

Finally, after having read the Bible myself, I shared it with a few of my personal friends. I told them to look and see. When they tell us in Islam to believe in Allah and the books of the past and the prophets of the past and the last day, this is one of those books that it is referring to. It includes the Torah, Zabour and Injil. I told them that we were born Muslim and we were told to believe in this book and for the last 14 centuries this book has been kept from us. I said we never had the right to read it. We were supposed to believe in it without knowing what it really says. This belief is meaningless. How can we believe in something that we have not seen, read or studied? This is useless and empty faith.

Anyway, out of the friends that got the Bible and read it, I think Satan used one of them to inform the Taliban.

When the Taliban were ruling in Kabul, they created a very powerful religious committee. It was called the Amre beh Maroof and Nahye az Monkar. This committee was composed of powerful Islamic mullahs that were well versed in the laws of Islam and in Sharia. They were the final authority in making judgments and pronouncing verdicts on the people, based on Sharia Law.

This committee had two functions, described by the two names. The first was, "Amre Beh Marrof," meaning, to dictate to people what must be done religiously and observe to make sure it is performed accordingly. The second name and function was, "Nahre az Monkar," which concerns things forbidden for Muslims. They policed society and set severe punishments for Muslims that do the forbidden acts. Having a Bible was one of those things that were forbidden for people, and there was punishment for owning, reading or studying it.

At this time, Kabul was in chaos with no industry or civil law, and it was full of terror. It was being ruled by the top Shiite and Sunni mullahs. The people were gagged from speaking out and barely permitted to breathe.

There was to be no TV or Radio or computer or pictures. They confiscated all the musical instruments and destroyed them. In one day, they put 6000-7000 TVs to fire. It was to the point that if they found a picture, a CD, a music tape in someone's house, they would confiscate it and punish the owner, since they were all part of the forbidden things. To be sure, this was genuine Islam.

In Islam there are the original, essential, elemental matters and the trivial and insignificant matters. Real Islam is the Taliban as well as Al Qaeda. The voice and face of true Islam is Hezbollah, Hamas and the revolution of the wicked, Ayatollah Khomeini of Iran. We can't say the Taliban, Al Qaeda, Hezbollah, Khomeini, Hamas, nor the Palestinian terrorists are not model Muslims. No, in actuality, they're acting according to the teaching of their books. Their teaching has ordered them to do these atrocities. True Muslims are sick and sentenced to do this thing. The Koran and the Hadith rule them. Mecca and Medina rule them, wherever they are around the world. But let's not go any further into that issue.

Instead, let's return to the main story. In the middle of the night I was asleep at home, when I heard a knocking at the door. I thought maybe it was a theif, so I got up to get dressed. But before I could get to the courtyard, I saw several criminal-like, governmental guards with guns, dressed in their religious garb, entering the house. They were of the committee of "Amre Beh Marrof" and "Nahre az Monkar," who were responsible to enforce the Islamic rules, and they entered my house as burglars.

Before I was able to open the door for them, they broke the door and entered the courtyard of my house. They introduced themselves as the committee members of the Islamic Ruling Taliban Government of Afghanistan. I said to them, "My brothers, what is the hurry, and why did you have to break down the door? I was on my way to open it. I would have welcomed you into my house. I would have been honored to have you in my place." But these men were very harsh, rough and unpleasant. They quickly attacked me and handcuffed me with hands behind my back. They used a chain of Omar and Ali, representing the two branches of Islam, Sunni and Shiite.

They said they had been informed that I started a house church in my home, and that a Kofre ("blasphemous") religion was in progress there. I said, "No, never, my brothers. No house church or any blasphemous things exist here. Let's go in and sit down and have a cup of tea together. My house is at your disposal. Look closely and see what I've been doing for humanity and what the followers of Ali and Omar are doing in this world."

After this, they ripped the house apart searching for any book that contained pictures, for picture albums, music, and cassette tapes. I also had a TV and a computer. They said they are all illegal in Islamic Sharia and that they are all Kophry ("blasphemous"). On the bed stand, beside my bed, I had several books of the poetry of Hafez, my favorite poet. Whenever I was stricken with sadness or worry, I would read these poems. I also had a Bible on my bed stand. When they saw these books, they first harassed me over the pictures that were in Hafez's books. The pictures were of beautiful ladies, hand drawn in miniature work for decoration to beautify the books, as publishers often do.

Then, they discovered the Bible. From here, the miracle takes shape. After they realized it was a Bible, they said, "Now we know that the information we received was accurate."

Now, in a very soft and gentle way, they requested that I confess the truth of my sin, and in so doing my conviction would be reduced. I was to confess with what foreign, infidel ("sinful") country I was in contact and what foreign and infidel ("sinful") church I was in relationship with. They asked, "From whom did you receive this book? And do you know how many Muslims have been invited into this ungodly, blasphemous religion? Take heed," they said, "of blasphemy." They were referring to Christianity and Judaism. They call them Kophry ("blasphemy"), unbelief, and infidelity ("sinfulness").

These were not ordinary people saying this. These are the *leaders* of Islam. I answered, "Please, if you permit, me it is a long story," and I relayed the story behind receiving the book through the bookstore business. I told them my business was books and education. I was serving my country by educating people, and at the same time, I had a bookstore to make a living and survive. I also told them that this book came into my possession completely accidentally. This Bible was mixed in with 6000 books that I had purchased from a business in Herat City near the border. The businessman that imported the book could not have known that it was there either, nor was I aware it was included with the books. I discovered it after I brought the remaining books into my library.

I read the book mainly because it says in Islam that we should believe in the four heavenly books. These four books are: first, the Koran, and also the Torah, the Injil (Gospels) and the Zabour (Psalms). I told them that I did not know that this book was a crime, that it was a sin, or that this was an ungodly book. They replied, "No, this book is definitely a blasphemous book. These books are abolished. Mohammed, the last prophet appeared and completed the godly religion. All the other heavenly books and all the old prophets and their laws and books, and everything they had has been abrogated. It is not permissible for a Muslim to study these books."

I asked them to please forgive me, that I certainly did not know that they were completely forbidden, and considered unclean, and that I was not supposed to read them. They said, "Oh no, you are not going to get away with this so easily." Consequently, they took the Bible, and from then on, as we say in Afghanistan, "Flowers rain on friends, but on me, stones rained."

They began to physically attack me, beating me on the head and legs. They broke my tooth as you can see, and my nose started bleeding. As they were doing these things to me, eventually I noticed that some of them were speaking Arabic and others, from Pakistan, were speaking in a Pakistani language. This was very painful to me. I was being beaten by an Arab. He was the one who was violating the sanctity of my home and my family. I never did anything to violate the land of the Arabs. I had never even gone there. But here, Arabs had come to my country of Afghanistan, and in the middle of the night came into my home and searched through all my things…

CHAPTER 4
I SURVIVED SHARIA LAW

They proceeded to blindfold me, pick me up, and put me in a car. They had several cars there. Since my eyes were blindfolded, I could not see anything. Also my hands were still tied behind my back.

They took me to their center in Kabul, to the headquarters of this committee from which they were leading and promoting the laws of Islam. There was another higher-up mullah sitting there. They put me and the Bible before him and accused, "This man has left his parents' religion and has become unclean. He is an apostate, and in this Islamic, Mohammedan country, he has started a home church. We have proof: we found this blasphemous book in his house."

That wicked and ignorant mullah also looked at the Bible and agreed and decreed that yes, this was true, that this book was blasphemy. He said, "This book cannot exist in an Islamic land, in a land in which the laws of the Koran and Mohammed rule." He also told me that my conviction could only be reduced if I divulged all the people that I had been involved with in this conspiracy. He wanted to know what other Muslims I had made unclean, their names and all the sources that provided the Bible for me. I was to reveal the network involved. In return for this, and the capture of this network they may be able to forgive and grant me amnesty rather than punishing me. They would punish the root cause, those responsible for bringing the Bible from outside the country into Islamic, Afghanistan. I had to reveal sources.

I told them, "I have told you all that I know. This is the truth." I said, "You can kill me if you want to, but I have nothing else to tell you. You can punish me if you want to, but you should know that if you torture me too much, since I have no strength to tolerate too much torture, I probably will lie to you in order to stop you from hurting me. In that case, I probably will give you some names of my friends and neighbors that had absolutely nothing to do with this. I can give you some lies now if you want, but if it'ss the truth you want, I've told that to you and there is nothing else to tell you."

They ordered me to be taken away; I was declared an infidel who had withheld secrets. They declared that my testimony revealed such, and that any Muslim that becomes a Christian is baptized in water. They stated that I, a Muslim-born person, was not legally permitted to leave his parent's religion or join another religion, and reasoned that the Bible was proof that I had received baptism either here, in Afghanistan, or outside the country. They also reasoned that I had chosen to believe in Christianity.

Therefore, their sentence was that I, as an unclean, evil, defiled and detestable person, according to the verses of the Koran, was to be taken and tortured little by little, so that one of two outcomes would be reached. Either, I would reveal sources to them, and tell them "the truth," or my completely unclean, dirty, defiled and apostate body—in their eyes—would be destroyed, killed, and thrown in the desert for the wild animals to eat.

According to them, this defiled body could not be buried, since the earth would not accept these unclean people.

So they blindfolded me again and put me in a small prison in the corner of the city of Kabul. Then, for the first time, they started to torture me. The first thing they did, as you can see from my first picture, was to cut off my left earlobe and have me lie there and suffer in pain.

Involved was another high-ranking mullah, along with a few Arabs that I assumed belonged to Al Qaeda and several Pakistani men that belonged to an organization called The Army of AL Tiyeb. These had come to Afghanistan for jihad. They are the ones that cut off my earlobe saying that this ear is unclean, because it has listened to the blasphemous book, the Bible. Then they poured acid into my ear.

Now you should ask any physician who knows about acid, its properties and effects, of what it will do when it is poured into the ear that is so close to the brain. This acid, which can put a hole in steel—imagine what it will do in the ear of a person, which is softer and thinner than a flower. When they put several drops in there. It felt like a volcanic eruption was taking place. I do not have the words to explain what this was like, as it is not an ordinary feeling; there is nothing like it. I used the term volcanic eruption, because I felt like my head was going to blow up. I fell into unconsciousness.

I spent more than 30 days in this prison. Then they took me to Kandahar, to some mountainous wilderness, where they had thousands of other people—women, men and children from all over Afghanistan—who had been accused of violating Sharia law in one form or another. They had been arrested by the committee, by Al Qaeda fighters in the north, or by the Afghani, Pakistani and Arab Taliban.

But most of them where less guilty than I. They would be interrogated for a few days and then they would be shot. But my crime was considered much worse, and they would not kill me, because they said "This body has received Christian baptism and therefore needs to be tortured little by little with acid and destroyed in this way. This unclean body must be removed from the earth. This is an apostate and corrupt body even to the point that the earth rejects it and it is in war with God.

You see, they accused me of being in war with God and corrupt on the earth.

So they repeated this torture of putting acid into my ears several times. And each time, I would fall into an unconscious state. Their intent was to gradually cut and destroy every part of my body. For that reason, one day, they cut out my left eye, saying that this eye is unclean and has read that blasphemous book, the

Bible.

My Christian brothers, my Jewish brothers, to read the Torah or the Gospels in the Islamic point of view, is blasphemous. They say it will defile you. How then can you work together with this fear and ignorance? Muslims, on the other hand, are free to practice what they want when they live in Christian or Jewish or other non-Muslim countries. They have their mosques and Islamic schools. They advertise and sell books and their Quran and everything that they want. They have no problems or restrictions put on them there. But in an Islamic country, to read one copy of the Gospels or Torah is considered an unforgivable crime. You become "defiled" if you read it.

So they took my eye out and put several drops of acid in the socket. In my eye socket, the acid and the blood and water were burning together. And, again, it felt like an explosion. And I again fell into unconsciousness. Several times they sprinkled salt and pepper on it also, and then they would bandage it up so the mixture would stay and burn in the socket.

They wanted to destroy this dirty and evil body from the brain out. But I was not destroyed. Always, the final point of each session was that I would pass out and go into a coma. But I would come back again.

The other tortures they put me through included putting acid over my body one place at a time followed by the sprinkling of salt and red pepper on it. This would cause the blood, water, and body fluid to fester together and dissolve with the acid as if melting together. But this flesh was not destroyed.

Our very first question was, "What is a miracle?" A miracle goes against natural law. Natural law says that a person could not possible survive all this contact with acid. Not even an animal such as an elephant or a camel could survive this. Against all odds, a miracle is performed only by God and according to his will and jurisdiction, not according to man's will. These things could not kill me even though they intended to do so. For here I am speaking to you right now, in my right mind.

Lastly, I will tell you of another one of the real crimes of Islam. They connected an electrical wire to my genitals. And they shocked me with electricity. They shocked me so many times that I felt like I was being thrown into the air and the sky was spinning around my head. Finally, they shocked me so much that blood was flowing profusely from my genitals. Again, one of them said we should not allow him to die so quickly, but he should be tortured more, so they stopped.

This body you seen in the pictures from the waist up is the real and live testimony of what they did to me. It is not made up of camera tricks or fabricated. They wounded my mouth and broke my tooth. They pounded nails into my head, though you can't see it clearly now. You can see my ear. You can ask any physician who understands science what the danger of acid on your body is. It is like an unimaginable fire, an unimaginable hell.

It was not only I that was being tortured, but also hundreds of other young girls that had been caught for not wearing the burka ("veil"). As punishment, they sprayed acid on their faces with the inquisition of, "Why did you leave the house without covering yourselves?" I saw this crime against humanity and against God.

I cannot explain everything in detail to you because of time. But let's go back to the question: what is a miracle? If one believes in God and His invisible power, and yet fails to believe that my being alive is a miracle of God and Jesus, it's just like denying the existence of the sun in the sky, like denying that the sun is shining and believing only in the darkness. It's being illogical and unbelieving.

For during that time, under those ugly and unpleasant tortures they were putting me through, I came to realize something. I thought to myself, "Oh You, the author of this Holy Bible, oh Jesus, You who according to this Book performed these miracles, and You who are the Son of God, You were born from the womb of the Virgin Mary, being born by the Holy Spirit, being born in human flesh, you who were lifted up on the cross and killed, who were buried and were resurrected three days later and went up into Heaven—if you are truly not a lie, if you are really God, and the Son of God, if this book is truly your word, please help me! They have taken me for the crime of having Your Bible. You know this. You know the whole story. If you are God, save me."

The miracle of God is this, that I am alive.

The other miracles that happened to me include how I was freed from jail and hell in 2001, when Kandahar was liberated from the Taliban by the American backed Afghani forces; how my family that I had sent away from Kabul many years earlier and had no information about, were found; how I was reunited with my wife and the kids; how we came to America through the UN; how I went through some treatment here and my health condition improved; how I fathered a daughter who is living with us right now in America even though the doctors had told me it would be impossible. Praise be to God.

CHAPTER 5
PICTORIAL ACCOUNT

From Hell To Heaven

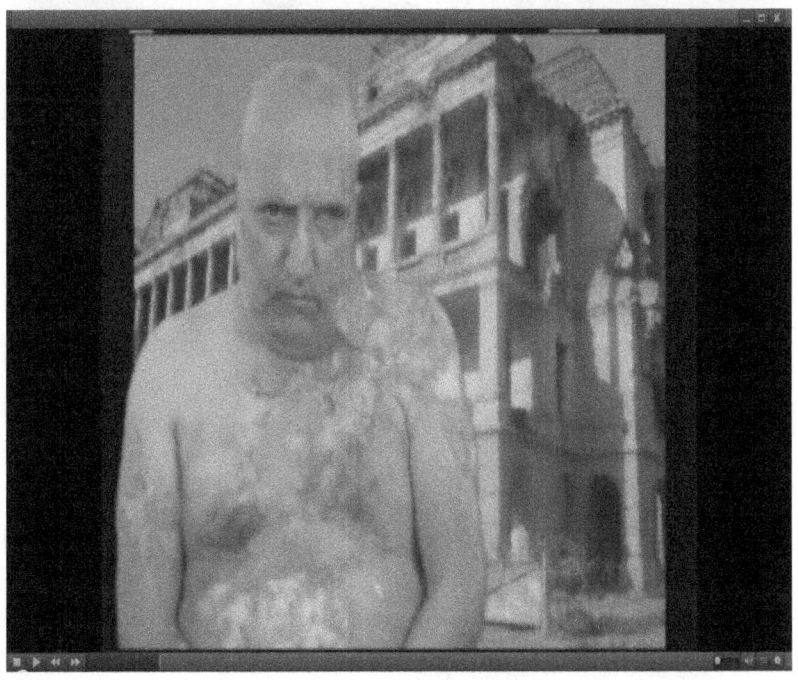

From Hell To Heaven

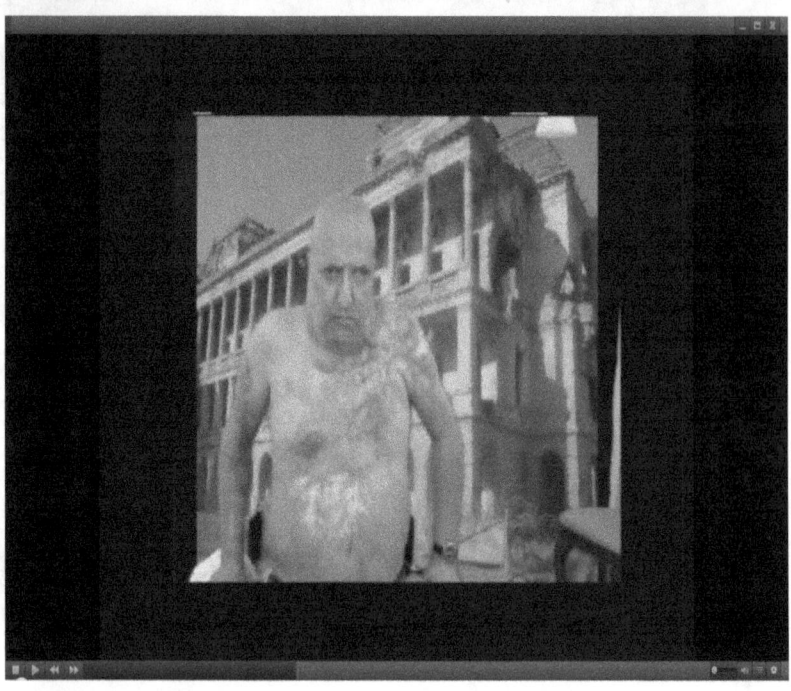

From Hell To Heaven

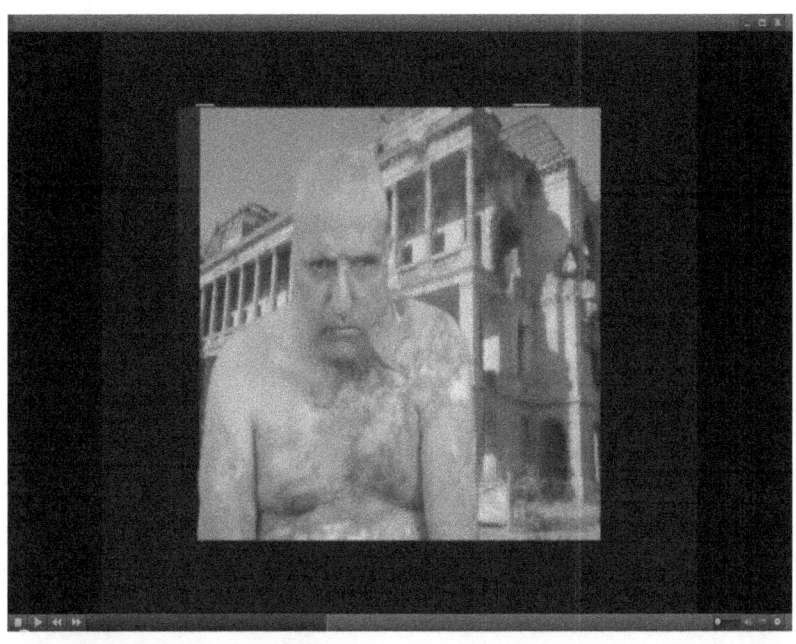

CHAPTER 6
PERSIAN POEM

اگر ایران به جز ویران‌سرا نیست   من این ویران‌سرا را دوست دارم.

اگر تاریخِ ما افسانه‌رنگ است   من این افسانه‌ها را دوست دارم.

نوای نایِ ما گر جان‌گداز است   من این نای و نوا را دوست دارم.

اگر آب و هوایَش دلنشین نیست   من این آب و هوا را دوست دارم.

به شوقِ خارِ صحراهای خشکَش   من این فرسوده‌پا را دوست دارم.

من این دلکش زمین را خواهم از جان   من این روشن‌سما را دوست دارم.

اگر بر من ز ایرانی رود زور،   من این زورآزما را دوست دارم.

اگر آلوده‌دامانید، اگر پاک   من ای مردم، شما را دوست دارم.

پژمان بختیاری

If Iran is not only demolished	I love demolished.
If our history is legend of colors	I love these legends.
If the sound of the trachea is heart-rending	I love the trachea and its tune.
If its weather or water is not pleasant	I love this weather and water.
The dry desert thorn passion	I love my challengers.
I like the attractive land of John	I love this bright sky.
If I used the Iranian force	I love my challengers.
If you are infected lap, if cleared	My people, I love you.

CHAPTER 7
RELIGION OF WAR

The following verses are from the Quran. They illustrate that the nature of this religion is not one of peace, but of war. I invite you to read for yourself and see. The verses are listed here in Persian (Farsi), Arabic, and English.

PERSIAN

8:12 در قلبها ترس میاندازیم
8:39 جنگ کنید تا دین فقط اسلام باشد
2:106 باطل سازی آیات
4:89 کفار را هر کجا پیدا کنید بکشید
4:91 پیشنهاد آشتی ندهید و دست از جنگ برندارید و آنها را بکشید
5:33 دستها وپاهای آنها را از جهت مخالف ببرید
2:217 کفر بدتر از قتل است
18:29 سرب مذاب بر سر آنها ریخته شود
18:30 مومنین پاداش عالی میگیرند
18:31 بروی آنها باغهای بهشتی نهر آب لباسهای حریر زربفت فداهم است
22:45 چه شهرها و چاها قصرهای بلندی که زیر و رو کردیم
9:29 آیه جزیه پول گرفتن از مسیحی زردشتی کلیمی با زور و حقارت آنها

9:5 در کمینگاه بنشینید و مشرکان را بکشید
9:33 پیغمبرش را فرستاد تا دین حق را بر همه ادیان چیره کند
9:31 ایشان کشیشان و خاخام های خود را شریک خدا میگیرند
9:32 روشنایی خدا را با سخنان خود خاموش کنند
47:4 وقتی کافران را پیدا میکنید گردن ایشان را بزنید
17:21 برخی از مردم را بر برخی دیگر ترجیح دادیم
33:60 ترا بر صد فتنه گران بر خواهیم انگیخت و سپس جز فقط اندکی در همسایگی تو نباشند(آنها را میکشم)
3:85 جز اسلام هیچ دینی قبول نخواهد شد

8:12   I will throw fear into the hearts
8:39   Fight until religion is all for Allah
2:106 We abrogate or cause to be forgotten any revelation
4:89   Kill them where you find them
4:91   No peace. Kill them wherever you find them
5:33   Have their hand and feet on alternate side cut off
2:217 Persecution is worse than killing!!
18:29 If they ask for showers, shower will be molten lead
18:30 If they believe they get good reward
18:31 For believers will be Garden of Eden, finest silk robes
22:45 How many township have we destroyed while it was sinful
9:29   Fight with people of Scripture (Jews & Christians, "People of the Book") until they pay the tribute, being brought low
9:5   Kill the idolaters whenever you find them
9:33   Allah has sent his messenger to prevail over all religion
9:30   Jews and Christians are perverse

9:31   They have taken as lords their rabbis and monks
9:32   They want to put out the light of Allah
47:4   When you meet disbelievers in battle, it is smiting of the necks
17:21 We prefer one above another
33:60 Hypocrites will be your neighbors no more
3:85   If anyone desired a religion other than Islam, never will it be accepted of him

---

ARABIC

الانفال 8:12

إِذْ يُوحِي رَبُّكَ إِلَى الْمَلآئِكَةِ أَنِّي مَعَكُمْ فَثَبِّتُواْ الَّذِينَ آمَنُواْ سَأُلْقِي فِي قُلُوبِ الَّذِينَ كَفَرُواْ الرَّعْبَ فَاضْرِبُواْ فَوْقَ الأَعْنَاقِ وَاضْرِبُواْ مِنْهُمْ كُلَّ بَنَانٍ

PERSIAN

هنگامی که پروردگارت به فرشتگان وحی می کرد که من با شما هستم پس کسانی را که ایمان آورده اند ثابت‌قدم بدارید به زودی در دل کافران وحشت‌خواهم افکند پس فراز گردنها را بزنید و همه سرانگشتانشان را قلم کنید

AL-ANFAL 8:12
Remember thy lord inspired the angels (with the message): "I am with you: give firmness to the believers: I will instill terror into the hearts of the unbelievers: smite ye above their necks and smite all their finger-tips off them."

ARABIC

الانفال 8:39

وَقَاتِلُوهُمْ حَتَّى لاَ تَكُونَ فِتْنَةٌ وَيَكُونَ الدِّينُ كُلُّهُ لِلّهِ فَإِنِ انتَهَوْاْ فَإِنَّ اللّهَ بِمَا يَعْمَلُونَ بَصِيرٌ

PERSIAN

و با آنان بجنگید تا فتنه‌ای بر جای نماند و دین یکسره از آن خدا گردد پس اگر [از کفر] بازایستند قطعا خدا به آنچه انجام می‌دهند بیناست

AL-ANFAL 8:39

And fight them on until there is no more tumult or oppression, and there prevail justice and faith in Allah altogether and everywhere; but if they cease, verily Allah doth see all that they do

---

ARABIC

البقره 2:106

مَا نَنسَخْ مِنْ آيَةٍ أَوْ نُنسِهَا نَأْتِ بِخَيْرٍ مِّنْهَا أَوْ مِثْلِهَا أَلَمْ تَعْلَمْ أَنَّ اللّهَ عَلَىَ كُلِّ شَيْءٍ قَدِيرٌ

PERSIAN

هر حکمی را نسخ کنیم یا آن را به [دست] فراموشی بسپاریم بهتر از آن یا مانندش را می‌آوریم مگر ندانستی که خدا بر هر کاری تواناست

AL-BAQARA 2:106

If we supersede any verse or cause it to be forgotten, we bring a better one or one similar. do you not know that Allah has power over all things!

ARABIC

النساآ 4:89

وَدُّواْ لَوْ تَكْفُرُونَ كَمَا كَفَرُواْ فَتَكُونُونَ سَوَاء فَلاَ تَتَّخِذُواْ مِنْهُمْ أَوْلِيَاء حَتَّىَ يُهَاجِرُواْ فِي سَبِيلِ اللّهِ فَإِن تَوَلَّوْاْ فَخُذُوهُمْ وَاقْتُلُوهُمْ حَيْثُ وَجَدتَّمُوهُمْ وَلاَ تَتَّخِذُواْ مِنْهُمْ وَلِيًّا وَلاَ نَصِيرًا

PERSIAN

همان گونه که خودشان کافر شده‌اند آرزو دارند [که شما نیز] کافر شوید تا با هم برابر باشید پس زنهار از میان ایشان برای خود دوستانی اختیار مکنید تا آنکه در راه خدا هجرت کنند پس اگر روی برتافتند هر کجا آنان را یافتید به اسارت بگیرید و بکشیدشان و از ایشان یار و یاوری برای خود مگیرید

AN-NISA 4:74

So let those who sell the worldly life for the everlasting life fight in the way of Allah, whoever fights in the way of Allah, and is killed or conquers, we shall give him a great wage.

ARABIC

النساآ 4:91

سَتَجِدُونَ آخَرِينَ يُرِيدُونَ أَن يَأْمَنُوكُمْ وَيَأْمَنُواْ

قَوْمَهُمْ كُلَّ مَا رُدُّواْ إِلَى الْفِتْنِةِ أُرْكِسُواْ فِيهَا فَإِن لَّمْ يَعْتَزِلُوكُمْ وَيُلْقُواْ إِلَيْكُمُ السَّلَمَ وَيَكُفُّواْ أَيْدِيَهُمْ فَخُذُوهُمْ وَاقْتُلُوهُمْ حَيْثُ ثَقِفْتُمُوهُمْ وَأُوْلَئِكُمْ جَعَلْنَا لَكُمْ عَلَيْهِمْ سُلْطَانًا مُّبِينًا

PERSIAN

به زودی گروهی دیگر را خواهید یافت که می‌خواهند از شما آسوده خاطر و از قوم خود [نیز] ایمن باشند هر بار که به فتنه بازگردانده شوند سر در آن فرو می‌برند پس اگر از شما کناره‌گیری نکردند و به شما پیشنهاد صلح نکردند و از شما دست برنداشتند هر کجا آنان را یافتید به اسارت بگیرید و بکشیدشان آنانند که ما برای شما علیه ایشان تسلطی آشکار قرار داده‌ایم

AN-NISA 4:91
You will find others desiring to be secure from you, and secure from their own nation. Whenever they are called back to sedition, they plunge into it. If they do not keep away from you and offer you peace, and restrain their hands, take them and kill them wherever you find them. Those, over them, we give you clear authority.

ARABIC

المايده 5:33

إِنَّمَا جَزَاءُ الَّذِينَ يُحَارِبُونَ اللهَ وَرَسُولَهُ وَيَسْعَوْنَ فِي الأَرْضِ فَسَادًا أَن يُقَتَّلُواْ أَوْ يُصَلَّبُواْ أَوْ تُقَطَّعَ أَيْدِيهِمْ وَأَرْجُلُهُم مِّنْ خِلَافٍ أَوْ يُنفَوْاْ مِنَ الأَرْضِ ذَلِكَ لَهُمْ خِزْيٌ فِي الدُّنْيَا وَلَهُمْ فِي الآخِرَةِ عَذَابٌ

عَظِيمٌ

PERSIAN

سزای کسانی که با [دوستداران] خدا و پیامبر او می‌جنگند و در زمین به فساد می‌کوشند جز این نیست که کشته شوند یا بر دار آویخته گردند یا دست و پایشان در خلاف جهت‌یکدیگر بریده شود یا از آن سرزمین تبعید گردند این رسوایی آنان در دنیاست و در آخرت عذابی بزرگ خواهند داشت

AL-MAEDA 5:33

The recompense of those who make war against Allah and his messenger and spread corruption in the land is that they are to be killed or crucified, or have their hand and a foot cut off on opposite sides, or be expelled from the land. For them is shame in this world and a great punishment in the everlasting life;

ARABIC

البقره 2:217

يَسْأَلُونَكَ عَنِ الشَّهْرِ الْحَرَامِ قِتَالٍ فِيهِ قُلْ قِتَالٌ فِيهِ كَبِيرٌ وَصَدٌّ عَن سَبِيلِ اللَّهِ وَكُفْرٌ بِهِ وَالْمَسْجِدِ الْحَرَامِ وَإِخْرَاجُ أَهْلِهِ مِنْهُ أَكْبَرُ عِندَ اللَّهِ وَالْفِتْنَةُ أَكْبَرُ مِنَ الْقَتْلِ وَلاَ يَزَالُونَ يُقَاتِلُونَكُمْ حَتَّىَ يَرُدُّوكُمْ عَن دِينِكُمْ إِنِ اسْتَطَاعُواْ وَمَن يَرْتَدِدْ مِنكُمْ عَن دِينِهِ فَيَمُتْ وَهُوَ كَافِرٌ فَأُوْلَئِكَ حَبِطَتْ أَعْمَالُهُمْ فِي الدُّنْيَا وَالآخِرَةِ وَأُوْلَئِكَ أَصْحَابُ النَّارِ هُمْ فِيهَا خَالِدُونَ

PERSIAN

از تو در باره ماهی که کارزار در آن حرام است می‌پرسند بگو کارزار در آن گناهی بزرگ و باز داشتن از راه خدا و کفر ورزیدن به او و باز داشتن از مسجدالحرام [=حج] و بیرون راندن اهل آن از آنجا نزد خدا [گناهی] بزرگتر و فتنه [=شرك] از کشتار بزرگتر است و آنان پیوسته با شما می‌جنگند تا اگر بتوانند شما را از دینتان برگردانند و کسانی از شما که از دین خود برگردند و در حال کفر بمیرند آنان کردارهایشان در دنیا و آخرت تباه می‌شود و ایشان اهل آتشند و در آن ماندگار خواهند بود

AL-BAQARA 2:217
They ask you about the sacred month and fighting in it. Say: 'to fight in this month is a grave (offense); but to bar others from the path of Allah, and disbelief in him, and the holy mosque, and to expel its inhabitants from it is greater with Allah. Dissension is greater than killing.' They will not cease to fight against you until they force you to renounce your religion, if they are able. But whosoever of you recants from his religion and dies an unbeliever, their works shall be annulled in this world and in the everlasting life, and those shall be the companions of hell, and there they shall live forever.

ARABIC

الكهف 31 18: 29

وَقُلِ الْحَقُّ مِن رَّبِّكُمْ فَمَن شَاءَ فَلْيُؤْمِن وَمَن شَاءَ فَلْيَكْفُرْ إِنَّا أَعْتَدْنَا لِلظَّالِمِينَ نَارًا أَحَاطَ بِهِمْ

سُرَادِقُهَا وَإِن يَسْتَغِيثُوا يُغَاثُوا بِمَاءٍ كَالْمُهْلِ يَشْوِي الْوُجُوهَ بِئْسَ الشَّرَابُ وَسَاءتْ مُرْتَفَقًا
30 إِنَّ الَّذِينَ آمَنُوا وَعَمِلُوا الصَّالِحَاتِ إِنَّا لَا نُضِيعُ أَجْرَ مَنْ أَحْسَنَ عَمَلًا
31 أُوْلَئِكَ لَهُمْ جَنَّاتُ عَدْنٍ تَجْرِي مِن تَحْتِهِمُ الْأَنْهَارُ يُحَلَّوْنَ فِيهَا مِنْ أَسَاوِرَ مِن ذَهَبٍ وَيَلْبَسُونَ ثِيَابًا خُضْرًا مِّن سُندُسٍ وَإِسْتَبْرَقٍ مُّتَّكِئِينَ فِيهَا عَلَى الْأَرَائِكِ نِعْمَ الثَّوَابُ وَحَسُنَتْ مُرْتَفَقًا

PERSIAN

29 و بگو حق از پروردگارتان [رسیده] است پس هر که بخواهد بگرود و هر که بخواهد انکار کند که ما برای ستمگران آتشی آماده کرده‌ایم که سراپرده‌هایش آنان را در بر می‌گیرد و اگر فریادرسی جویند به آبی چون مس گداخته که چهره‌ها را بریان می‌کند یاری می‌شوند وه چه بد شرابی و چه زشت جایگاهی است

30 کسانی که ایمان آورده و کارهای شایسته کرده‌اند [بدانند که] ما پاداش کسی را که نیکوکاری کرده است تباه نمی‌کنیم

31 آنانند که بهشتهای عدن به ایشان اختصاص دارد که از زیر [قصرها]شان جویبارها روان است در آنجا با دستبندهایی از طلا آراسته می‌شوند و جامه‌هایی سبز از پرنیان نازک و حریر ستبر می‌پوشند در آنجا بر سریرها تکیه می‌زنند چه خوش پاداش و نیکو تکیه‌گاهی

AL-KAHF 18:29-31

Say: 'this is the truth from your lord. let whosoever

will, believe, and whosoever will, disbelieve it. ' for the harm-doers, we have prepared a fire, the pavilion of which encompasses them. When they cry out for relief, they shall be showered with water as hot as molten copper, which will scald their faces; how evil a drink, and how evil a resting place!

30 as for those who believe and do good works we do not waste the wage of whosoever does good works.

31 those, they shall live in the gardens of Eden, underneath which rivers flow. They shall be adorned with bracelets of gold and arrayed in green garments of silk, and brocade, reclining therein on couches; how excellent is their reward and how fine is their resting place!

ARABIC

الحج 22:45

فَكَأَيِّن مِّن قَرْيَةٍ أَهْلَكْنَاهَا وَهِيَ ظَالِمَةٌ فَهِيَ خَاوِيَةٌ عَلَى عُرُوشِهَا وَبِئْرٍ مُّعَطَّلَةٍ وَقَصْرٍ مَّشِيدٍ

PERSIAN

و چه بسیار شهرها را که ستمکار بودند هلاکشان کردیم و [اینك] آن [شهرها] سقفهایش فرو ریخته است و [چه بسیار] چاههای متروك و كوشكهای افراشته را

AL-HAJJ 22:45

How many a village we have destroyed in its harm-doing, so that it lies fallen upon its turrets, and how many an abandoned well, and empty palace!

ARABIC

التوبه 9:29

قَاتِلُواْ الَّذِينَ لاَ يُؤْمِنُونَ بِاللّهِ وَلاَ بِالْيَوْمِ الآخِرِ وَلاَ يُحَرِّمُونَ مَا حَرَّمَ اللّهُ وَرَسُولُهُ وَلاَ يَدِينُونَ دِينَ الْحَقِّ مِنَ الَّذِينَ أُوتُواْ الْكِتَابَ حَتَّى يُعْطُواْ الْجِزْيَةَ عَن يَدٍ وَهُمْ صَاغِرُونَ

PERSIAN

با کسانی از اهل کتاب که به خدا و روز بازپسین ایمان نمی‌آورند و آنچه را خدا و فرستاده‌اش حرام گردانیده‌اند حرام نمی‌دارند و متدین به دین حق نمی‌گردند کارزار کنید تا با [کمال] خواری به دست‌خود جزیه دهند

AL-TAWBA 9:29

Fight those who neither believe in Allah nor the last day, who do not forbid what Allah and his messenger have forbidden, and do not embrace the religion of the truth, being among those who have been given the book (Bible and the Torah), until they pay tribute out of hand and have been humiliated.

ARABIC

التوبه 9:5

فَإِذَا انسَلَخَ الأَشْهُرُ الْحُرُمُ فَاقْتُلُواْ الْمُشْرِكِينَ حَيْثُ وَجَدتُّمُوهُمْ وَخُذُوهُمْ وَاحْصُرُوهُمْ وَاقْعُدُواْ لَهُمْ كُلَّ مَرْصَدٍ فَإِن تَابُواْ وَأَقَامُواْ الصَّلاَةَ وَآتَوُاْ الزَّكَاةَ فَخَلُّواْ سَبِيلَهُمْ إِنَّ اللّهَ غَفُورٌ رَّحِيمٌ

PERSIAN

پس چون ماه‌های حرام سپری شد مشرکان را هر کجا یافتید بکشید و آنان را دستگیر کنید و به محاصره درآورید و در هر کمینگاهی به کمین آنان بنشینید پس اگر توبه کردند و نماز برپا داشتند و زکات دادند راه برایشان گشاده گردانید زیرا خدا آمرزنده مهربان است

AL-TAWBA 9:5

When the sacred months are over, slay the idolaters wherever you find them. Take them and confine them, then lie in ambush everywhere for them. if they repent and establish the prayer and pay the obligatory charity, let them go their way. Allah is forgiving and the most merciful.

ARABIC

التوبه 9:33

هُوَ الَّذِي أَرْسَلَ رَسُولَهُ بِالْهُدَى وَدِينِ الْحَقِّ لِيُظْهِرَهُ عَلَى الدِّينِ كُلِّهِ وَلَوْ كَرِهَ الْمُشْرِكُونَ

PERSIAN

او کسی است که پیامبرش را با هدایت و دین درست فرستاد تا آن را بر هر چه دین است پیروز گرداند هر چند مشرکان خوش نداشته باشند

AL-TAWBA 9:33

It is he who has sent forth his messenger with guidance and the religion of truth to uplift it above every religion, no matter how much the idolaters hate it.

ARABIC

التوبة 9:30 32

وَقَالَتِ الْيَهُودُ عُزَيْرٌ ابْنُ اللّهِ وَقَالَتْ النَّصَارَى الْمَسِيحُ ابْنُ اللّهِ ذَلِكَ قَوْلُهُم بِأَفْوَاهِهِمْ يُضَاهِؤُونَ قَوْلَ الَّذِينَ كَفَرُواْ مِن قَبْلُ قَاتَلَهُمُ اللّهُ أَنَّى يُؤْفَكُونَ 31اتَّخَذُواْ أَحْبَارَهُمْ وَرُهْبَانَهُمْ أَرْبَابًا مِّن دُونِ اللّهِ وَالْمَسِيحَ ابْنَ مَرْيَمَ وَمَا أُمِرُواْ إِلاَّ لِيَعْبُدُواْ إِلَهًا وَاحِدًا لاَّ إِلَهَ إِلاَّ هُوَ سُبْحَانَهُ عَمَّا يُشْرِكُونَ 32 يُرِيدُونَ أَن يُطْفِؤُواْ نُورَ اللّهِ بِأَفْوَاهِهِمْ وَيَأْبَى اللّهُ إِلاَّ أَن يُتِمَّ نُورَهُ وَلَوْ كَرِهَ الْكَافِرُونَ

PERSIAN

30و یهود گفتند عزیر پسر خداست و نصاری گفتند مسیح پسر خداست این سخنی است [باطل] که به زبان می‌آورند و به گفتار کسانی که پیش از این کافر شده‌اند شباهت دارد خدا آنان را بکشد چگونه [از حق] بازگردانده می‌شوند

31اینان دانشمندان و راهبان خود و مسیح پسر مریم را به جای خدا به الوهیت گرفتند با آنکه مأمور نبودند جز اینکه خدایی یگانه را بپرستند که هیچ معبودی جز او نیست منزه است او از آنچه [با وی] شریک می‌گردانند

32می‌خواهند نور خدا را با سخنان خویش خاموش کنند ولی خداوند نمی‌گذارد تا نور خود را کامل کند هر چند کافران را خوش نیاید

AL-TAWBA 9:30-32

The Jews say Ezra is the son of Allah, while the Christians (who follow Paul) say the Messiah is the son of Allah. Such are their assertions, by which they imitate those who disbelieved before. Allah fights them! How perverted are they!

31 They take their rabbis and monks as lords besides Allah, and the Messiah, son of Mary, though they were ordered to worship but one God, there is no God except he. Exalted is he above that they associate with him!

32 They desire to extinguish the light of Allah with their mouths; but Allah seeks only to perfect his light, though the unbelievers hate it.

ARABIC

محمد 47:4

فَإِذا لَقِيتُمُ الَّذِينَ كَفَرُوا فَضَرْبَ الرِّقَابِ حَتَّى إِذَا أَثْخَنتُمُوهُمْ فَشُدُّوا الْوَثَاقَ فَإِمَّا مَنًّا بَعْدُ وَإِمَّا فِدَاءً حَتَّى تَضَعَ الْحَرْبُ أَوْزَارَهَا ذَلِكَ وَلَوْ يَشَاءُ اللهُ لَانتَصَرَ مِنْهُمْ وَلَكِن لِّيَبْلُوَ بَعْضَكُم بِبَعْضٍ وَالَّذِينَ قُتِلُوا فِي سَبِيلِ اللهِ فَلَن يُضِلَّ أَعْمَالَهُمْ

PERSIAN

پس چون با کسانی که کفر ورزیده‌اند برخورد کنید گردنها[یشان] را بزنید تا چون آنان را [در کشتار] از پای درآوردید پس [اسیران را] استوار در بند کشید سپس یا [بر آنان] منت نهید [و آزادشان کنید] و یا فدیه [و عوض از ایشان بگیرید] تا در جنگ اسلحه بر زمین گذاشته شود این است [دستور خدا] و اگر خدا می‌خواست از ایشان انتقام می‌کشید ولی [فرمان پیکار داد] تا برخی از شما را به وسیله برخی [دیگر] بیازماید و کسانی که در راه خدا کشته شده‌اند هرگز کارهایشان را ضایع نمی‌کند

MUHAMMAD 47:4

Therefore, when you meet the unbelievers smite their necks, then, when you have killed many of them, tie the bonds. Then, either free them by grace or ransom until war shall lay down its loads, in this way, it shall be. Had Allah willed, he would have been victorious over them; except that he might test you, the one by the means of others. As for those who are killed in the way of Allah, he will not let their works to go astray.

ARABIC

الإسراء 17:16

وَإِذَا أَرَدْنَا أَن نُّهْلِكَ قَرْيَةً أَمَرْنَا مُتْرَفِيهَا فَفَسَقُواْ فِيهَا فَحَقَّ عَلَيْهَا الْقَوْلُ فَدَمَّرْنَاهَا تَدْمِيرًا

PERSIAN

و چون بخواهیم شهری را هلاك كنیم خوشگذرانانش را وا می‌داریم تا در آن به انحراف [و فساد] بپردازند و در نتیجه عذاب بر آن [شهر] لازم گردد پس آن را [یکسره] زیر و زبر کنیم

AL-ISRA 17:16

When we decide to destroy a population, we (first) send a definite order to those among them who are given the good things of this life and yet transgress; so that the word is proved true against them: then (it is) we destroy them utterly.

ARABIC

الإسراء 17:21

انظُرْ كَيْفَ فَضَّلْنَا بَعْضَهُمْ عَلَى بَعْضٍ وَلَلْآخِرَةُ أَكْبَرُ دَرَجَاتٍ وَأَكْبَرُ تَفْضِيلًا

PERSIAN

ببین چگونه بعضی از آنان را بر بعضی دیگر برتری داده‌ایم و قطعا درجات آخرت و برتری آن بزرگتر و بیشتر است

AL-ISRA 17:21

See how we have bestowed more on some than on others; but verily the hereafter is more in rank and gradation and more in excellence.

ARABIC

الأحزاب 33:60

لَئِن لَّمْ يَنتَهِ الْمُنَافِقُونَ وَالَّذِينَ فِي قُلُوبِهِم مَّرَضٌ وَالْمُرْجِفُونَ فِي الْمَدِينَةِ لَنُغْرِيَنَّكَ بِهِمْ ثُمَّ لَا يُجَاوِرُونَكَ فِيهَا إِلَّا قَلِيلًا

PERSIAN

اگر منافقان و کسانی که در دلهایشان مرضی هست و شایعه‌افکنان در مدینه [از کارشان] باز نایستند تو را سخت بر آنان مسلط می‌کنیم تا جز [مدتی] اندک در همسایگی تو نپایند

AL-AHZAB 33:60

If the hypocrites and those who have a disease in their hearts, and those who make a commotion in the city do not desist, we will surely urge you against them. Then they will be your neighbors for only a little (while),

---

ARABIC
آل عمران 3:85

وَمَن يَبْتَغِ غَيْرَ الإِسْلاَمِ دِينًا فَلَن يُقْبَلَ مِنْهُ وَهُوَ فِي الآخِرَةِ مِنَ الْخَاسِرِينَ

PERSIAN
و هر که جز اسلام دینی [دیگر] جوید هرگز از وی پذیرفته نشود و وی در آخرت از زیانکاران است

HOUSE OF 'IMRAN 3:85
If anyone desires a religion other than Islam (submission to Allah), never will it be accepted of him; and in the hereafter he will be in the ranks of those who have lost (all spiritual good).

CHAPTER 8
OPPRESSION OF WOMEN

PERSIAN

ستمگری بر زنان

2:223 زنها کشتزار شما هستند. از هر دری به کشتزار خود وارد شوید(تشویق به لواط کاری)

4:15 زنهای زانکار را در منزل حبس کنید تا مرگ آنان برسد

33:59 آیه حجاب

4:34 کتک زدن زنها

4:51 نوبت زنها را میتوانی رعایت نکنی

4:24 زنهایی که در جنگ اسیر میکنی بتو هلال هستند

4:4 نوش جان کردن مهریه زنها

33:52 زن بیشتر نمیتوانی مگر کنیز باشند

33:50 به محمد اجازه داده میشود که با هر زن مومنه ازدواج کند

4:3 چهار زن گرفتن

65:4 وعده سه ماه است حتی برای دخترهایی که هنوز بسن قاعدگی نرسیده اند (تشویق ازدواج با دختر بچه ها)

33:5 اسم فامیل خودتان را روی بچه های سر راهیتان نگذارید(عدم تشویق برداشتن بچه سر راهی)

Oppressing Women

2:223 Women are a planting place (a tilth), go into them as you will (encouraging sodomy)

4:15 Women who are guilty of lewdness confine them until death

33:59 Tell women to draw their cloaks round them (Islamic outfit)

4:34 Men excel the women; if you fear rebellion, beat them

33:51 it is not a sin for profit to disregard his women's turn

4:24 you are not to marry married women, except war captured ones

4:4 Give women free gift of marriage, except war captured ones

33:52 You are not to take any more women, unless you marry slaves

33:50 It is allowed for profit to marry any believing woman, if she wants to

65:4 Waiting period will be 3 months for those who

have or have to reached menstruation!! (encouraging child marriage)
33:5 Do not put your family name on adopted child!! (discouraging child adoption)

ARABIC

البقرة 2:233

نِسَآؤُكُمْ حَرْثٌ لَّكُمْ فَأْتُواْ حَرْثَكُمْ أَنَّى شِئْتُمْ وَقَدِّمُواْ لِأَنفُسِكُمْ وَاتَّقُواْ اللّهَ وَاعْلَمُواْ أَنَّكُم مُّلاَقُوهُ وَبَشِّرِ الْمُؤْمِنِينَ

PERSIAN

زنان شما کشتزار شما هستند پس از هر جا [و هر گونه] که خواهید به کشتزار خود [در]آیید و آنها را برای خودتان مقدم دارید و از خدا پروا کنید و بدانید که او را دیدار خواهید کرد و مؤمنان را [به این دیدار] مژده ده

Al Baghareh 2:233
Your wives are as a tilth ("like a field to plant seed") unto you; so approach your tilth when or how ye will; but do some good act for your souls beforehand; and fear Allah. and know that ye are to meet him (in the hereafter), and give (these) good tidings to those who believe.

ARABIC

4:15 النساء

وَاللَّاتِي يَأْتِينَ الْفَاحِشَةَ مِن نِّسَائِكُمْ فَاسْتَشْهِدُواْ عَلَيْهِنَّ أَرْبَعةً مِّنكُمْ فَإِن شَهِدُواْ فَأَمْسِكُوهُنَّ فِي الْبُيُوتِ حَتَّىَ يَتَوَفَّاهُنَّ الْمَوْتُ أَوْ يَجْعَلَ اللَّهُ لَهُنَّ سَبِيلًا

PERSIAN

و از زنان شما کسانی که مرتکب زنا می‌شوند چهار تن از میان خود [مسلمانان] بر آنان گواه گیرید پس اگر شهادت دادند آنان [=زنان] را در خانه‌ها نگاه دارید تا مرگشان فرا رسد یا خدا راهی برای آنان قرار دهد

If any of your women commit indecency, call in four witnesses from among yourselves against them, if they testify, confine them to their houses till death overtakes them or till Allah makes for them a way.

ARABIC

33:59 الأحزاب

يَا أَيُّهَا النَّبِيُّ قُل لِّأَزْوَاجِكَ وَبَنَاتِكَ وَنِسَاء الْمُؤْمِنِينَ يُدْنِينَ عَلَيْهِنَّ مِن جَلَابِيبِهِنَّ ذَلِكَ أَدْنَى أَن يُعْرَفْنَ فَلَا يُؤْذَيْنَ وَكَانَ اللَّهُ غَفُورًا رَّحِيمًا

PERSIAN

ای پیامبر به زنان و دخترانت و به زنان مؤمنان بگو پوششهای خود را بر خود فروتر گیرند این برای آنکه شناخته شوند و مورد آزار قرار نگیرند [به احتیاط] نزدیکتر است و خدا آمرزنده مهربان است

O prophet! Tell thy wives and daughters, and the believing women, that they should cast their outer garments over their persons (when abroad): that is most convenient, that they should be known (as such) and not molested. and Allah is oft-forgiving, most merciful

---

ARABIC

4:34 النساء

الرِّجَالُ قَوَّامُونَ عَلَى النِّسَاءِ بِمَا فَضَّلَ اللهُ بَعْضَهُمْ عَلَى بَعْضٍ وَبِمَا أَنفَقُوا مِنْ أَمْوَالِهِمْ فَالصَّالِحَاتُ قَانِتَاتٌ حَافِظَاتٌ لِّلْغَيْبِ بِمَا حَفِظَ اللهُ وَاللَّاتِي تَخَافُونَ نُشُوزَهُنَّ فَعِظُوهُنَّ وَاهْجُرُوهُنَّ فِي الْمَضَاجِعِ وَاضْرِبُوهُنَّ فَإِنْ أَطَعْنَكُمْ فَلاَ تَبْغُوا عَلَيْهِنَّ سَبِيلًا إِنَّ اللهَ كَانَ عَلِيًّا كَبِيرًا

PERSIAN

مردان سرپرست زنانند به دلیل آنکه خدا برخی از ایشان را بر برخی برتری داده و [نیز] به دلیل آنکه از اموالشان خرج می‌کنند پس زنان درستکار فرمانبردارند [و] به پاس آنچه خدا [برای آنان] حفظ کرده اسرار [شوهران خود] را حفظ می‌کنند و زنانی

را که از نافرمانی آنان بیم دارید [نخست] پندشان دهید و [بعد] در خوابگاه‌ها از ایشان دوری کنید و [اگر تاثیر نکرد] آنان را ترک کنید پس اگر شما را اطاعت کردند [دیگر] بر آنها هیچ راهی [برای سرزنش] مجویید که خدا والای بزرگ است

Men are the protectors and maintainers of women, because Allah has given the one more (strength) than the other, and because they support them from their means. Therefore the righteous women are devoutly obedient, and guard in (the husband's) absence what Allah would have them guard. as to those women on whose part ye fear disloyalty and ill-conduct, admonish them (first), (next), refuse to share their beds, (and last) leave them; but if they return to obedience, seek not against them means (of annoyance): for Allah is most high, great (above you all).

ARABIC

الأحزاب 33:51

تُرْجِي مَن تَشَاءُ مِنْهُنَّ وَتُؤْوِي إِلَيْكَ مَن تَشَاءُ وَمَنِ ابْتَغَيْتَ مِمَّنْ عَزَلْتَ فَلَا جُنَاحَ عَلَيْكَ ذَلِكَ أَدْنَى أَن تَقَرَّ أَعْيُنُهُنَّ وَلَا يَحْزَنَّ وَيَرْضَيْنَ بِمَا آتَيْتَهُنَّ كُلُّهُنَّ وَاللَّهُ يَعْلَمُ مَا فِي قُلُوبِكُمْ وَكَانَ اللَّهُ عَلِيمًا حَلِيمًا

PERSIAN

نوبت هر کدام از آن از زنها را که می‌خواهی به تاخیر انداز و هر کدام را که می‌خواهی پیش خود جای ده و بر تو باکی نیست که هر کدام را که ترک کرده‌ای [دوباره] طلب کنی این نزدیکتر است برای اینکه چشمانشان روشن گردد و دلتنگ نشوند و همگی‌شان به آنچه به آنان داده‌ای خشنود گردند و آنچه در دلهای شماست خدا می‌داند و خدا همواره دانای بردبار است

Thou mayest defer (the turn of) any of them that thou pleasest, and thou mayest receive any thou pleasest: and there is no blame on thee if thou invite one whose (turn) thou hadst set aside. This were nigher to the cooling of their eyes, the prevention of their grief, and their satisfaction - that of all of them - with that which thou hast to give them: and Allah knows (all) that is in your hearts: and Allah is all-knowing, most forbearing

---

ARABIC

النساء 4:24

وَالْمُحْصَنَاتُ مِنَ النِّسَاء إِلاَّ مَا مَلَكَتْ أَيْمَانُكُمْ كِتَابَ اللّهِ عَلَيْكُمْ وَأُحِلَّ لَكُم مَّا وَرَاء ذَلِكُمْ أَن تَبْتَغُواْ بِأَمْوَالِكُم مُّحْصِنِينَ غَيْرَ مُسَافِحِينَ فَمَا اسْتَمْتَعْتُم بِهِ مِنْهُنَّ فَآتُوهُنَّ أُجُورَهُنَّ فَرِيضَةً وَلاَ جُنَاحَ عَلَيْكُمْ فِيمَا تَرَاضَيْتُم بِهِ مِن بَعْدِ الْفَرِيضَةِ إِنَّ اللّهَ كَانَ عَلِيمًا حَكِيمًا

PERSIAN

و زنان شوهردار [نیز بر شما حرام شده است] به استثنای زنانی که مالک آنان شده‌اید [این] فریضه الهی است که بر شما مقرر گردیده است و غیر از این [زنان نامبرده] برای شما حلال است که [زنان دیگر را] به وسیله اموال خود طلب کنید در صورتی که پاکدامن باشید و زناکار نباشید و زنانی را که متعه کرده‌اید مهرشان را به عنوان فریضه‌ای به آنان بدهید و بر شما گناهی نیست که پس از مقرر با یکدیگر توافق کنید مسلما خداوند دانای حکیم است

Also (prohibited are) women already married, except those whom your right hands possess: thus hath Allah ordained (prohibitions) against you: except for these, all others are lawful, provided ye seek (them in marriage) with gifts from your property,- desiring chastity, not lust, seeing that ye derive benefit from them, give them their dowers (at least) as prescribed; but if, after a dower is prescribed, agree mutually (to vary it), there is no blame on you, and Allah is all-knowing, all-wise

---

ARABIC

4:4 النساء

وَآتُواْ النِّسَاءَ صَدُقَاتِهِنَّ نِحْلَةً فَإِن طِبْنَ لَكُمْ عَن شَيْءٍ مِّنْهُ نَفْسًا فَكُلُوهُ هَنِيئًا مَّرِيئًا

PERSIAN

و مهر زنان را به عنوان هدیه‌ای از روی طیب خاطر به ایشان

بدهید و اگر به میل خودشان چیزی از آن را به شما واگذاشتند آن را حلال و گوارا بخورید

And give the women (on marriage) their dower as a free gift; but if they, of their own good pleasure, remit any part of it to you, take it and enjoy it with right good cheer

---

ARABIC

33:52 الأحزاب

لَا يَحِلُّ لَكَ النِّسَاءُ مِن بَعْدُ وَلَا أَن تَبَدَّلَ بِهِنَّ مِنْ أَزْوَاجٍ وَلَوْ أَعْجَبَكَ حُسْنُهُنَّ إِلَّا مَا مَلَكَتْ يَمِينُكَ وَكَانَ اللَّهُ عَلَىٰ كُلِّ شَيْءٍ رَّقِيبًا

PERSIAN

از این پس دیگر [گرفتن] زنان و نیز اینکه به جای آنان زنان دیگری بر تو حلال نیست هر چند زیبایی آنها برای تو مورد پسند افتد به استثنای کنیزان و خدا همواره بر هر چیزی مراقب است

It is not lawful for thee (to marry more) women after this, nor to change them for (other) wives, even though their beauty attract thee, except any thy right hand should possess (as handmaidens): and Allah doth watch over all things.

ARABIC

33:50 الأحزاب

يَا أَيُّهَا النَّبِيُّ إِنَّا أَحْلَلْنَا لَكَ أَزْوَاجَكَ اللَّاتِي آتَيْتَ أُجُورَهُنَّ وَمَا مَلَكَتْ يَمِينُكَ مِمَّا أَفَاء اللَّهُ عَلَيْكَ وَبَنَاتِ عَمِّكَ وَبَنَاتِ عَمَّاتِكَ وَبَنَاتِ خَالِكَ وَبَنَاتِ خَالَاتِكَ اللَّاتِي هَاجَرْنَ مَعَكَ وَامْرَأَةً مُّؤْمِنَةً إِن وَهَبَتْ نَفْسَهَا لِلنَّبِيِّ إِنْ أَرَادَ النَّبِيُّ أَن يَسْتَنكِحَهَا خَالِصَةً لَّكَ مِن دُونِ الْمُؤْمِنِينَ قَدْ عَلِمْنَا مَا فَرَضْنَا عَلَيْهِمْ فِي أَزْوَاجِهِمْ وَمَا مَلَكَتْ أَيْمَانُهُمْ لِكَيْلَا يَكُونَ عَلَيْكَ حَرَجٌ وَكَانَ اللَّهُ غَفُورًا رَّحِيمًا

PERSIAN

ای پیامبر ما برای تو آن همسرانی را که مهرشان را دادهای حلال کردیم و [کنیزانی] را که خدا از غنیمت جنگی در اختیار تو قرار داده و دختران عمویت و دختران عمههایت و دختران دایی تو و دختران خالههایت که با تو مهاجرت کردهاند و زن مؤمنی که خود را [داوطلبانه] به پیامبر ببخشددر صورتی که پیامبر بخواهد او را به زنی گیرد [این ازدواج از روی بخشش] ویژه توست نه دیگر مؤمنان ما نیك میدانیم که در مورد زنان و کنیزانشان چه بر آنان مقرر کردهایم تا برای تو مشکلی پیش نیاید و خدا همواره آمرزنده مهربان است

O prophet! We have made lawful to thee thy wives to whom thou hast paid their dowers; and those whom thy right hand possesses out of the prisoners of war whom Allah has assigned to thee; and daughters of thy paternal uncles and aunts, and daughters of thy maternal uncles and aunts, who migrated (from

Mecca) with thee; and any believing woman who dedicates her soul to the prophet if the prophet wishes to wed her; this only for thee, and not for the believers (at large); we know what we have appointed for them as to their wives and the captives whom their right hands possess;- in order that there should be no difficulty for thee. And Allah is oft-forgiving, most merciful.

ARABIC

65:4 الطلاق

وَاللَّائِي يَئِسْنَ مِنَ الْمَحِيضِ مِن نِّسَائِكُمْ إِنِ ارْتَبْتُمْ فَعِدَّتُهُنَّ ثَلَاثَةُ أَشْهُرٍ وَاللَّائِي لَمْ يَحِضْنَ وَأُولَاتُ الْأَحْمَالِ أَجَلُهُنَّ أَن يَضَعْنَ حَمْلَهُنَّ وَمَن يَتَّقِ اللَّهَ يَجْعَل لَّهُ مِنْ أَمْرِهِ يُسْرًا

PERSIAN

و آن زنان شما که از خون‌دیدن [ماهانه] نومیدند اگر شک دارید [که خون می‌بینند یا نه] عده آنان سه ماه است و [دخترانی] که [هنوز] خون ندیده‌اند [نیز عده‌شان سه ماه است] و زنان آبستن مدتشان این است که وضع حمل کنند و هر کس از خدا پروا دارد [خدا] برای او در کارش تسهیلی فراهم سازد

Such of your women as have passed the age of monthly courses, for them the prescribed period, if ye have any doubts, is three months, and for those who have no courses (it is the same): for those who carry (life within their wombs), their period is until they deliver their burdens: and for those who fear Allah, he will make their path easy.

ARABIC

33:5 الأحزاب

ادْعُوهُمْ لِآبَائِهِمْ هُوَ أَقْسَطُ عِندَ اللَّهِ فَإِن لَّمْ تَعْلَمُوا آبَاءهُمْ فَإِخْوَانُكُمْ فِي الدِّينِ وَمَوَالِيكُمْ وَلَيْسَ عَلَيْكُمْ جُنَاحٌ فِيمَا أَخْطَأْتُم بِهِ وَلَكِن مَّا تَعَمَّدَتْ قُلُوبُكُمْ وَكَانَ اللَّهُ غَفُورًا رَّحِيمًا

PERSIAN

آنان را به [نام] پدرانشان بخوانید که این نزد خدا عادلانه‌تر است و اگر پدرانشان را نمی‌شناسید پس برادران دینی و موالی شمایند و در آنچه اشتباها مرتکب آن شده‌اید بر شما گناهی نیست ولی در آنچه دلهایتان عمد داشته است [مسؤولید] و خداست که همواره آمرزنده مهربان است

33:5

Call them by (the names of) their fathers: that is just in the sight of Allah. but if ye know not their father's (names, call them) your brothers in faith, or your mullahs. but there is no blame on you if ye make a mistake therein: (what counts is) the intention of your hearts: and Allah is oft-returning, most merciful.

CHAPTER 9
THE LORD'S PRAYER

PERSIAN

انجیل متی

فصل 6 آیات

ای پدر ما که در آسمانی،
نام تو مقدّس باد.
10 پادشاهی تو بیاید
ارادهٔ تو، چنانکه در آسمان انجام می‌شود،
بر زمین نیز به انجام رسد.
11 نان روزانهٔ ما را امروز به ما عطا فرما
12 و قرضهای ما را ببخش،
چنانکه ما نیز قرضداران خود را می‌بخشیم.
13 و ما را در آزمایش میاور،
بلکه از آن شرور رهاییمان ده.
زیرا پادشاهی و قدرت و جلال، تا ابد از آنِ توست. آمین.

The Lord's Prayer

Our Father in heaven, may your name be set apart as holy.
Your kingdom come, your will be done, on earth, as it is in heaven.
Give us this day our daily bread, and forgive us our debts, as we also forgive our debtors.
And you would not bring us into temptation, but deliver us from evil one.
For the kingdom, the power and the glory are yours, now and forever. Amen.

CHAPTER 10
THE APOSTLES CREED/NICENE CREED
325 AD

اعتقادنامه مسیحی

من ایمان دارم به خدای پدر قادر مطلق، خالق آسمان و زمین،
و به پسر یگانه او خداوند ما عیسی مسیح که به واسطۀ روح القدس
در رحم قرار گرفت و از مریم باکره متولد شد و در حکومت پنطیوس
پیلاطس الم کشید و مصلوب شده بمرد و مدفون گردید، و به عالم
ارواح نزول کرد و در روز سوم از مردگان برخاست، به آسمان
صعود نموده و به دست راست خدای پدر قادر مطلق نشسته است
و از آنجا خواهد آمد و زندگان و مردگان را داوری نماید و من ایمان
دارم به روح القدس و به کلیسای مقدس جامع و به شرکت مقدسین

و به آمرزش گناهان و به قیامت ابدان و به حیات جاودان. آمین

The Apostles Creed (Nicene Creed)

I believe in God, the Father Almighty,
the Creator of heaven and earth,
and in Jesus Christ, His only Son, our Lord:
Who was conceived of the Holy Spirit,
born of the Virgin Mary,
suffered under Pontius Pilate,
was crucified, died, and was buried.
He descended into hell.
The third day He arose again from the dead.
He ascended into heaven and sits at the right hand of
God the Father Almighty,
whence He shall come to judge the living and the
dead. I believe in the Holy Spirit,
the holy universal church,
the communion of saints,
the forgiveness of sins,
the resurrection of the body,
and life everlasting. Amen.

CHAPTER 11
UNIVERSAL DECLARATION OF HUMAN RIGHTS

PERSIAN

اعلامیه جهانی حقوق بشر

مقدمه

از آنجا که شناسایی حیثیت ذاتی کلیه اعضای خانواده بشری و حقوق یکسان و انتقال ناپذیر آنان اساس آزادی و عدالت و صلح را در جهان تشکیل می دهد ، از آنجا که عدم شناسایی وتحقیر حقوق بشر منتهی به اعمال وحشیانه ای گردیده است که روح بشریت را به عصیان واداشته و ظهور دنیایی که در آن افراد بشر در بیان عقیده آزاد و از ترس و فقر فارغ باشند به عنوان بالاترین آمال بشر اعلام شده است ، از آنجا که اساساً حقوق انسانی را باید با اجرای قانون حمایت کرد تا بشر به عنوان آخرین علاج به قیام بر ضد ظلم و فشار مجبور نگردد ، از آنجا که اساساً لازم است توسعه روابط دوستانه بین الملل را مورد تشویق قرار داد ، از آنجا که مردم ملل متحد ایمان خود را به حقوق اساسی بشر و مقام و ارزش فرد انسانی و تساوی حقوق مرد و زن مجدداً در منشور اعلام کرده اند و تصمیم راسخ گرفته اند که به پیشرفت اجتماعی

کمک کنند و در محیطی آزادتر وضع زندگی بهتری به وجود آورند ، از آنجاکه دولتهای عضو متعهد شده اند که احترام جهانی و رعایت واقعی حقوق بشر و آزادی های اساسی را با همکاری سازمان ملل متحد تامین کنند ، از آنجا که حسن تفاهم مشترک نسبت به این حقوق و آزادیها برای اجرای کامل این تعهد کمال اهمیت را دارد ، مجمع عمومی این اعلامیه جهانی حقوق بشر را آرمان مشترکی برای تمام مردم و کلیه ملل اعلام می کند تا جمیع افراد و کلیه ارکان اجتماع این اعلامیه را دائماً مد نظر داشته باشند و مجاهدت کنند که بوسیله تعلیم و تربیت احترام این حقوق و آزادی ها توسعه یابد و با تدابیر تدریجی ملی و بین المللی ، شناسایی و اجرای واقعی و حیاتی آنها ، چه در میان خود ملل عضو و چه در بین مردم کشورهایی که در قلمرو آنها می باشند ، تامین گردد .

ماده اول : تمام افراد بشر آزاد به دنیا می آیند و از لحاظ حیثیت و حقوق با هم برابرند . همه دارای عقل و وجدان می باشند و باید با یکدیگر با روح برادری رفتار کنند .

ماده دوم :

1) هر کس میتواند بدون هیچ تمایز   خصوصاً از حیث رنگ ، جنس ، نژاد ، مذهب ، عقیده سیاسی یا هر عقیده ی دیگر و همچنین ملیت و وضع اجتماعی ، ثروت ، ولادت یا هر موقعیت دیگر ، از تمام حقوق و کلیه ی آزادی هایی که در اعلامیه حاضر ذکر شده است بهره مند گردد .

2) به علاوه هیچ تبعیضی به عمل نخواهد آمد که مبتنی بر وضع سیاسی ، اداری و قضایی یا بین المللی کشور یا سرزمینی که

شخص به آن تعلق دارد . خواه اين كشور مستقل ، تحت قيوميت يا خود مختار بوده و يا حاكميت آن به شكلي محدود شده باشد .

ماده سوم : هر كس حق زندگي ، آزادي و امنيت شخصي دارد .

ماده چهارم : احدي را نمي توان در بردگي نگاه داشت و داد و ستد بردگان به هر شكلي كه باشد ممنوع است .

ماده پنجم : احدي را نمي توان تحت شكنجه يا مجازات يا رفتاري قرار داد كه ظالمانه يا خلاف انسانيت و شئون انساني يا موهن باشد .

ماده ششم : هر كس حق دارد كه شخصيت حقوقي او در همه جا به عنوان يك انسان در مقابل قانون شناخته شود .

ماده هفتم : همه در برابر قانون مساوي هستند و حق دارند بدون تبعيض و بالسويه از حمايت قانون برخوردار شوند . همه حق دارند در مقابل هر تبعيضي كه ناقض اعلاميه حاضر باشد و هر تحريكي كه براي اعمال چنين تبعيضي انجام شود از حمايت قانون برخوردار شوند .

ماده هشتم : در برابر اعمالي كه حقوق اساسي فرد را مورد تجاوز قرار دهد و آن حقوق به وسيله ي قانون اساسي و يا قانون ديگري براي او شناخته شده باشد ، هر كس حق رجوع موثر به محاكم ملي صالحه را دارد .

ماده نهم : احدي را نمي توان خودسرانه توقيف ، حبس يا تبعيد نمود .

ماده دهم : هر كس با مساوات كامل حق دارد كه دعوايش بوسيله

ي دادگاه مستقل و بي طرف ، منصفانه و علناً رسيدگي شود و چنين دادگاهي درباره ي حقوق و الزامات او و يا هر اتهام جزائي كه به او وارد شده باشد تصميم بگيرد .

ماده يازدهم :

1) هر كس كه به بزهكاري متهم شده باشد بي گناه محسوب خواهد شد تا وقتي كه در جريان يك دعواي عمومي كه كليه تضمين هاي لازم جهت دفاع او تامين شده باشد ، تقصير او قانوناً محرز گردد .

2) هيچ كس براي انجام يا عدم انجام عملي كه در موقع ارتكاب ، آن عمل به موجب حقوق ملي يا بين المللي جرم شناخته نمي شده است محكوم نخواهد شد . به همين طريق هيچ مجازاتي شديد تر از آنچه كه در موقع ارتكاب جرم بدان تعلق ميگرفت در باره ي احدي اجرا نخواهد شد .

ماده دوازدهم : احدي در زندگي خصوصي ، امور خانوادگي ، اقامتگاه يا مكاتبات خود ، نبايد مورد مداخله هاي خود سرانه واقع شود و شرافت و اسم و رسمش نبايد مورد حمله قرار گيرد . هر كس حق دارد در مقابل اينگونه مداخلات و حملات مورد حمايت قانون قرار گيرد .

ماده سيزدهم :

1) هر كس حق دارد كه در داخل هر كشوري آزادانه عبور و مرور كند و محل اقامت خود را انتخاب كند .

2) هر كس حق دارد هر كشوري از جمله كشور خود را ترك كند يا به آن بازگردد .

ماده چهاردهم :

1) هركس حق دارد در مقابل شكنجه ، آزار و تعقيب پناهگاهي جستجو كند و در كشورهاي ديگر پناه گزيند .

2) در مواردي كه تعقيب واقعاً مبتني به جرم عمومي و غير سياسي يا رفتارهايي مغاير با اصول و مقاصد ملل متحد باشد نميتوان از اين حق استفاده كرد .

ماده پانزدهم :

1) هر كس حق دارد كه داراي تابعيت باشد .

2) احدي را نمي توان خودسرانه از تابعيت خود يا از حق تغيير تابعيت محروم كرد .

ماده شانزدهم :

1) هر زن و مرد بالغي حق دارند بدون هيچگونه محدوديت از نظر نژاد ، مليت ، تابعيت يا مذهب با يكديگر زناشويي كنند و تشكيل خانواده دهند . در تمام مدت زناشويي و هنگام انحلال آن ، زن و شوهر در كليه امور مربوط به ازدواج داراي حقوق مساوي مي باشند .

2) ازدواج بايد با رضايت كامل و آزادانه زن و مرد واقع شود .

ماده هفدهم :

1) هر كس منفرداً يا بطور دسته جمعي حق مالكيت دارد .

2) احدي را نمي توان خودسرانه از حق مالكيت محروم نمود .

ماده هیجدهم : هر کس حق دارد که از آزادي فکر ، وجدان و مذهب بهره مند شود . این حق متضمن آزادي تغییر مذهب یا عقیده و نیز متضمن آزادي اظهار عقیده و ایمان میباشد و همچنین شامل تعلیمات مذهبي و اجراي مراسم دیني است . هر کس میتواند از این حقوق منفرداً اجتماعاً و به طور خصوصي یا عمومي برخوردار شود.

ماده نوزدهم : هر کس حق آزادي عقیده و بیان دارد و حق مزبور شامل آنست که از داشت عقاید خود بیم و اضطرابي نداشته باشد و در کسب اطلاعات و افکار و در اخذ و انتشار آن به تمام وسایل ممکن و بدون ملاحظات مرزي آزاد باشد .

ماده بیستم :

1) هر کس حق دارد آزادانه مجامع و جمعیتهاي مسالمت آمیز تشکیل دهد .

2) هیچکس را نمیتوان مجبور به شرکت در اجتماعي کرد .

ماده بیست و یکم :

1) هر کس حق دارد در اداره ي امور عمومي کشور خود ، خواه مستقیماً و خواه از طریق نمایندگاني که آزادانه انتخاب شده باشند شرکت جوید .

2) هر کس حق دارد با تساوي شرایط به مشاغل عمومي کشور خود نایل آید .

3) اساس و منشاء قدرت حکومت اراده ي مردم است . این اراده باید به وسیله ي انتخاباتي ابراز گردد که از روي صداقت و

بطور ادواري صورت پذيرد . انتخابات بايد عمومي و با رعايت مساوات باشد و با راي مخفي يا طريقه اي نظير آن انجام گيرد كه آزادي راي را تضمين نمايد .

ماده بيست و دوم : هر كس به عنوان عضو اجتماع حق امنيت اجتماعي دارد و مجاز است بوسيله ي مساعي ملي و همكاري بين المللي حقوق اقتصادي و اجتماعي و فرهنگي خود را كه لازمه ي مقام و نمو آزادانه ي شخصيت اوست با رعايت تشكيلات و منابع هر كشور بدست آورد .

ماده بيست وسوم :

1) هر كس حق دارد كار كند ، كار خود را آزادانه انتخاب نمايد ، شرايط منصفانه و رضايت بخشي براي كار خود خواستار باشد و در مقابل بيكاري مورد حمايت قرار گيرد .

2) همه حق دارند بدون هيچ تبعيضي در مقابل كار مساوي اجرت مساوي دريافت كنند .

3) هر كس كه كار مي كند به مزد منصفانه و رضايت بخشي ذيحق ميشود كه زندگي او و خانواده اش را موافق شئون انساني تامين كند و آنرا در صورت لزوم با هر نوع وسايل ديگر حمايت اجتماعي تكميل نمايد .

4) هر كس حق دارد براي دفاع از منافع خود با ديگران اتحاديه تشكيل دهد يا در اتحاديه ها شركت كند .

ماده بيست و چهارم : هر كس حق استراحت و فراغت و تفريح دارد و به خصوص به محدوديت معقول ساعات كار و مرخصي هاي ادواري با اخذ حقوق ذيحق ميباشد .

ماده بيست و پنجم :

1) هر كس حق دارد كه سطح زندگاني او ، سلامتي و رفاه خود و خانواده اش را از حيث خوراك و مسكن و مراقبتهاي پزشكي و خدمات لازم اجتماعي تامين كند و همچنين حق دارد كه در مواقع بيكاري ، بيماري ، نقص اعضاء ، بيوگي ، پيري يا تمام موارد ديگري كه به عللي خارج از اراده ي انسان وسايل امرار معاش از دست رفته باشد ، از شرايط آبرومندانه ي زندگي برخوردار شود .

2) مادران و كودكان حق دارند از كمك و مراقبت مخصوصي بهره مند شوند . كودكان چه بر اثر ازدواج و چه بدون ازدواج به دنيا آمده باشند ، حق دارند كه همه از يكنوع حمايت اجتماعي برخوردار شوند .

ماده بيست وششم :

1) هر كس حق دارد كه از آموزش و پرورش بهره مند شود . آموزش و پرورش لااقل تا حدودي كه مربوط به تعليمات ابتدايي و اساسي است بايد رايگان باشد . آموزش ابتدايي اجباري است . آموزش حرفه اي بايد عموميت پيدا كند و آموزش عالي بايد با شرايط تساوي كامل به روي همه باز باشد تا همه بنا به استعداد خود بتوانند از آن بهره گيرند .

2) آموزش و پرورش بايد طوري هدايت شود كه شخصيت انساني هر فرد را به حد كمال رشد آن برساند و احترام حقوق و آزادي هاي بشر را تقويت كند . آموزش و پرورش بايد حس تفاهم ، گذشت و احترام به عقيده ي مخالف و دوستي بين تمام ملل و جمعيتهاي نژادي يا مذهبي و همچنين توسعه ي فعاليتهاي ملل

متحد را در راه حفظ صلح تسهیل نماید .

3) پدر و مادر در انتخاب نوع آموزش و پرورش فرزندان خود نسبت به دیگران اولویت دارند .

ماده بیست و هفتم :

1) هر کس حق دارد آزادانه در زندگی فرهنگی اجتماع شرکت کند ، از فنون و هنر ها بهره گیرد و در پیشرفت علمی و فوائد آن سهیم باشد .

2) هر کس حق دارد از حمایت منافع مادی و معنوی آثار علمی ، فرهنگی یا هنری خود برخوردار شود .

ماده بیست و هشتم : هر کس حق دارد برقراری نظمی را بخواهد که از لحاظ اجتماعی و بین المللی ، حقوق و آزادی هایی را که در این اعلامیه ذکر گردیده است تامین کند و آنها را به مورد اجرا گذارد .

ماده بیست و نهم :

1) هر کس در مقابل آن جامعه ای وظیفه دارد که رشد آزاد و کامل شخصیت او را میسر کند .

2) هر کس در اجرای حقوق و استفاده از آزادی های خود فقط تابع محدودیت هایی است که به وسیله قانون و منحصراً به منظور تامین ، شناسایی و مراعات حقوق و آزادی های دیگران و برای رعایت صحیح مقتضیات اخلاقی و نظم عمومی و رفاه همگانی در شرایط یک جامعه ی دمکراتیک وضع گردیده است .

ماده سی ام : هیچ یک از مقررات اعلامیه حاضر نباید طوری

تفسیر شود که متضمن حقی برای دولت ، جمعیت یا فردی باشد که به موجب آن بتوانند هر یک از حقوق و آزادیهای مندرج در این اعلامیه را از بین ببرند یا در راه آن فعالیتی نمایند .

PREAMBLE

Whereas recognition of the inherent dignity and of the equal and inalienable rights of all members of the human family is the foundation of freedom, justice and peace in the world,

Whereas disregard and contempt for human rights have resulted in barbarous acts which have outraged the conscience of mankind, and the advent of a world in which human beings shall enjoy freedom of speech and belief and freedom from fear and want has been proclaimed as the highest aspiration of the common people,

Whereas it is essential, if man is not to be compelled to have recourse, as a last resort, to rebellion against tyranny and oppression, that human rights should be protected by the rule of law,

Whereas it is essential to promote the development of friendly relations between nations,

Whereas the peoples of the United Nations have in the Charter reaffirmed their faith in fundamental human rights, in the dignity and worth of the human person and in the equal rights of men and women and have determined to promote social progress and better standards of life in larger freedom,

Whereas Member States have pledged themselves to achieve, in co-operation with the United Nations, the promotion of universal respect for and observance of human rights and fundamental freedoms,

Whereas a common understanding of these rights

and freedoms is of the greatest importance for the full realization of this pledge,

Now, Therefore THE GENERAL ASSEMBLY proclaims THIS UNIVERSAL DECLARATION OF HUMAN RIGHTS as a common standard of achievement for all peoples and all nations, to the end that every individual and every organ of society, keeping this Declaration constantly in mind, shall strive by teaching and education to promote respect for these rights and freedoms and by progressive measures, national and international, to secure their universal and effective recognition and observance, both among the peoples of Member States themselves and among the peoples of territories under their jurisdiction.

Article 1.
- All human beings are born free and equal in dignity and rights. They are endowed with reason and conscience and should act towards one another in a spirit of brotherhood.

Article 2.
- Everyone is entitled to all the rights and freedoms set forth in this Declaration, without distinction of any kind, such as race, colour, sex, language, religion, political or other opinion, national or social origin, property, birth or other status. Furthermore, no distinction shall be made on the basis of the political, jurisdictional or international status of the country or territory to which a person belongs, whether it be independent, trust, non-self-governing or under any other limitation of sovereignty.

Article 3.
- Everyone has the right to life, liberty and security of person.

Article 4.
- No one shall be held in slavery or servitude; slavery and the slave trade shall be prohibited in all their forms.

Article 5.
- No one shall be subjected to torture or to cruel, inhuman or degrading treatment or punishment.

Article 6.
- Everyone has the right to recognition everywhere as a person before the law.

Article 7.
- All are equal before the law and are entitled without any discrimination to equal protection of the law. All are entitled to equal protection against any discrimination in violation of this Declaration and against any incitement to such discrimination.

Article 8.
- Everyone has the right to an effective remedy by the competent national tribunals for acts violating the fundamental rights granted him by the constitution or by law.

Article 9.
- No one shall be subjected to arbitrary arrest, detention or exile.

Article 10.
- Everyone is entitled in full equality to a fair and public hearing by an independent and impartial tribunal, in the determination of his rights and obligations and of any criminal

charge against him.

Article 11.
- (1) Everyone charged with a penal offence has the right to be presumed innocent until proved guilty according to law in a public trial at which he has had all the guarantees necessary for his defence.
- (2) No one shall be held guilty of any penal offence on account of any act or omission which did not constitute a penal offence, under national or international law, at the time when it was committed. Nor shall a heavier penalty be imposed than the one that was applicable at the time the penal offence was committed.

Article 12.
- No one shall be subjected to arbitrary interference with his privacy, family, home or correspondence, nor to attacks upon his honour and reputation. Everyone has the right to the protection of the law against such interference or attacks.

Article 13.
- (1) Everyone has the right to freedom of movement and residence within the borders of each state.
- (2) Everyone has the right to leave any country, including his own, and to return to his country.

Article 14.
- (1) Everyone has the right to seek and to enjoy in other countries asylum from persecution.
- (2) This right may not be invoked in the case of prosecutions genuinely arising from non-political crimes or from acts contrary to the purposes and principles of the United Nations.

Article 15.
- (1) Everyone has the right to a nationality.
- (2) No one shall be arbitrarily deprived of his nationality nor denied the right to change his nationality.

Article 16.
- (1) Men and women of full age, without any limitation due to race, nationality or religion, have the right to marry and to found a family. They are entitled to equal rights as to marriage, during marriage and at its dissolution.
- (2) Marriage shall be entered into only with the free and full consent of the intending spouses.
- (3) The family is the natural and fundamental group unit of society and is entitled to protection by society and the State.

Article 17.
- (1) Everyone has the right to own property alone as well as in association with others.
- (2) No one shall be arbitrarily deprived of his property.

Article 18.
- Everyone has the right to freedom of thought, conscience and religion; this right includes freedom to change his religion or belief, and freedom, either alone or in community with others and in public or private, to manifest his religion or belief in teaching, practice, worship and observance.

Article 19.
- Everyone has the right to freedom of opinion and expression; this right includes freedom to hold opinions without interference and to seek, receive and impart information and ideas

through any media and regardless of frontiers.

Article 20.
- (1) Everyone has the right to freedom of peaceful assembly and association.
- (2) No one may be compelled to belong to an association.

Article 21.
- (1) Everyone has the right to take part in the government of his country, directly or through freely chosen representatives.
- (2) Everyone has the right of equal access to public service in his country.
- (3) The will of the people shall be the basis of the authority of government; this will shall be expressed in periodic and genuine elections which shall be by universal and equal suffrage and shall be held by secret vote or by equivalent free voting procedures.

Article 22.
- Everyone, as a member of society, has the right to social security and is entitled to realization, through national effort and international co-operation and in accordance with the organization and resources of each State, of the economic, social and cultural rights indispensable for his dignity and the free development of his personality.

Article 23.
- (1) Everyone has the right to work, to free choice of employment, to just and favourable conditions of work and to protection against unemployment.
- (2) Everyone, without any discrimination, has the right to equal pay for equal work.

- (3) Everyone who works has the right to just and favourable remuneration ensuring for himself and his family an existence worthy of human dignity, and supplemented, if necessary, by other means of social protection.
- (4) Everyone has the right to form and to join trade unions for the protection of his interests.

Article 24.
- Everyone has the right to rest and leisure, including reasonable limitation of working hours and periodic holidays with pay.

Article 25.
- (1) Everyone has the right to a standard of living adequate for the health and well-being of himself and of his family, including food, clothing, housing and medical care and necessary social services, and the right to security in the event of unemployment, sickness, disability, widowhood, old age or other lack of livelihood in circumstances beyond his control.
- (2) Motherhood and childhood are entitled to special care and assistance. All children, whether born in or out of wedlock, shall enjoy the same social protection.

Article 26.
- (1) Everyone has the right to education. Education shall be free, at least in the elementary and fundamental stages. Elementary education shall be compulsory. Technical and professional education shall be made generally available and higher education shall be equally accessible to all on the basis of merit.

- (2) Education shall be directed to the full development of the human personality and to the strengthening of respect for human rights and fundamental freedoms. It shall promote understanding, tolerance and friendship among all nations, racial or religious groups, and shall further the activities of the United Nations for the maintenance of peace.
- (3) Parents have a prior right to choose the kind of education that shall be given to their children.

Article 27.
- (1) Everyone has the right freely to participate in the cultural life of the community, to enjoy the arts and to share in scientific advancement and its benefits.
- (2) Everyone has the right to the protection of the moral and material interests resulting from any scientific, literary or artistic production of which he is the author.

Article 28.
- Everyone is entitled to a social and international order in which the rights and freedoms set forth in this Declaration can be fully realized.

Article 29.
- (1) Everyone has duties to the community in which alone the free and full development of his personality is possible.
- (2) In the exercise of his rights and freedoms, everyone shall be subject only to such limitations as are determined by law solely for the purpose of securing due recognition and respect for the rights and freedoms of others

and of meeting the just requirements of morality, public order and the general welfare in a democratic society.
- (3) These rights and freedoms may in no case be exercised contrary to the purposes and principles of the United Nations.

Article 30.
- Nothing in this Declaration may be interpreted as implying for any State, group or person any right to engage in any activity or to perform any act aimed at the destruction of any of the rights and freedoms set forth herein.

CHAPTER 12
CYRUS THE GREAT

Cyrus II; Kourosh in Persian; Kouros in Greek

Artistic portrait of Cyrus the Great

Cyrus (580-529 BC) was the first Achaemenid

Emperor.[1] He founded Persia by uniting the two, original Iranian Tribes- the Medes and the Persians. Although he was known to be a great conqueror, who at one point controlled one of the greatest Empires ever seen, he is best remembered for his unprecedented tolerance and magnanimous attitude towards those he defeated.

Upon his victory over the Medes, he founded a government for his new kingdom, incorporating both Median and Persian nobles as civilian officials. The conquest of Asia Minor completed, he led his armies to the eastern frontiers. Hyrcania and Parthia were already part of the Median Kingdom. Further east, he conquered Drangiana, Arachosia, Margiana and Bactria. After crossing the Oxus, he reached the Jaxartes, where he built fortified towns with the object of defending the farthest frontier of his kingdom against nomadic tribes of Central Asia.

The victories to the east led him again to the west and sounded the hour for attack on Babylon and Egypt. When he conquered Babylon, he did so to cheers from the Jewish Community, who welcomed him as a liberator- he allowed the Jews to return to the promised Land. He showed great forbearance and respect towards the religious beliefs and cultural traditions of other races. These qualities earned him the respect and homage of all the people over whom he ruled.

---

[1] http://www.iranchamber.com/history/achaemenids/achaemenids.php

Bas-Relief of Cyrus the Great, in Pasargad, Iran

The victory over Babylonia expressed all the facets of the policy of conciliation which Cyrus had followed until then. He presented himself not as a conqueror, but a liberator and the legitimate successor to the crown. He also declared the first Charter of Human Rights[2] known to mankind. He took the title

---

[2] http://www.iranchamber.com/history/cyrus/cyrus_charter.php

of "King of Babylon and King of the Land". Cyrus had no thought of forcing conquered people into a single mold, and had the wisdom to leave unchanged the institution of each kingdom he attached to the Persian Crown. In 539 BCE he allowed more than 40,000 Jews to leave Babylon and return to Palestine. This step was in line with his policy to bring peace to Mankind. A new wind was blowing from the east, carrying away the cries and humility of defeated and murdered victims, extinguishing the fires of sacked cities, and liberating nations from slavery.

Cyrus was upright, a great leader of men, generous and benevolent. The Hellenes, whom he conquered regarded him as 'Law-giver' and the Jews as "the anointed (or "chosen/appointed") of the Lord."

Prior to his death, he founded a new capital city at Pasargade in Fars. and had established a government for his Empire. He appointed a governor (satrap) to represent him in each province, however the administration, legislation, and cultural activities of each province was the responsibility of the Satraps. According to Xenophon Cyrus is also reputed to have devised the first postal system, (Achaemenid achievements). His doctrines were adopted by the future emperors of the Achaemenian dynasty.

GOD RAISES UP A KING

God's instrument, Cyrus, came to power sometime around 550 B.C. They called him "Cyrus the Great." Read about him in Isaiah 41:2-3; 44:28; 45:3; 45:13; 46:10-11; 48:14-15. Look at the job description God gave Cyrus in Isaiah 44:28; 45:13; 48:14-15: a. To free the captive Jews, b. To help rebuild Jerusalem, c. To cause the foundations of the temple to be laid, d. To punish Babylon.

Cyrus freed the Jewish people to return to their homeland: Isaiah 45:13.

Cyrus enabled the rebuilding of Jerusalem as predicted: Isaiah 44:28 and 45:13.

Cyrus helped to rebuild the temple foundation: We see in II Chronicles 36:23, Cyrus acknowledging that God had specifically appointed him for the task.

Cyrus punished Babylon: In Isaiah 48:14-15 he is referred to as "the Lord's chosen ally" who carried out His purpose against Babylon.

THE CYLINDER OF CYRUS

متن استخراج شده از استوانه کورش، خطوط ۱۵ تا ۲۱.

متن استوانه[3]

استوانهٔ کوروش، استوانه‌ای از جنس خاک رس[4] است که از دو قسمت تشکیل شده‌است؛ تکهٔ اول، همان قطعهٔ اصلی گل‌نوشته است که هرمز رسام آن را کشف کرده بود و در ۳۵ خط نوشته‌شده و تکهٔ دوم شامل خط‌های ۳۶ تا ۴۵

---

[3] https://fa.wikipedia.org/w/index.php?title=%D8%A7%D8%B3%D8%AA%D9%88%D8%A7%D9%86%D9%87_%DA%A9%D9%88%D8%B1%D9%88%D8%B4&action=edit&section=4

[4] https://fa.wikipedia.org/wiki/%D8%B1%D8%B3

می‌شود و در کلکسیون بابلی دانشگاه ییل[5] توسط پاول ریچارد برگر پیدا شد.[6] درازای این استوانه ۲۲٫۸۶ سانتی‌متر و پهنای آن ۱۱ سانتی‌متر است و به زبان اکدی[7] (بابلی نو[8]) نوشته شده‌است. این گل‌نوشته به‌شکل استوانه‌ای است که دو انتهای این استوانه باریک‌تر و در وسط کمی بَرآمده‌است. این استوانه شامل ۴۵ خط می‌شود که روی‌هم‌رفته حدود ۲۰ سطر از آن کاملاً شکسته‌شده و امروزه در دست نیست و سه سطر ابتدایی آن نیز تقریباً به طور کامل شکسته‌اند و قابل خواندن نیستند.[9]

تکهٔ اول این استوانه، پس از کشف به موزهٔ بریتانیا انتقال یافت و با شمارهٔ BM 90920 در این موزه نگهداری می‌شود.[10] تکهٔ دوم که قطعهٔ کوچکی به‌اندازهٔ ۸٫۶ در ۵٫۶ سانتی‌متر است، سطرهای ۳۶ تا ۴۵ گل‌نوشته را شامل می‌شود. این قطعهٔ کوچک با شمارهٔ NBC 2504 در مجموعهٔ دانشگاه ییل کشور ایالات متحدهٔ آمریکا[11] نگهداری می‌شد

---

[5] https://fa.wikipedia.org/wiki/%D8%AF%D8%A7%D9%86%D8%B4%DA%AF%D8%A7%D9%87_%DB%8C%DB%8C%D9%84

[6] https://fa.wikipedia.org/wiki/%D8%A7%D8%B3%D8%AA%D9%88%D8%A7%D9%86%D9%87_%DA%A9%D9%88%D8%B1%D9%88%D8%B4_-_cite_note-14

[7] https://fa.wikipedia.org/wiki/%D8%B2%D8%A8%D8%A7%D9%86_%D8%A7%DA%A9%D8%AF%DB%8C

[8] https://fa.wikipedia.org/wiki/%D8%AF%D8%A8%DB%8C%D8%B1%D9%87_%D9%85%DB%8C%D8%AE%DB%8C_%D8%A7%DA%A9%D8%AF%DB%8C

[9] https://fa.wikipedia.org/wiki/%D8%A7%D8%B3%D8%AA%D9%88%D8%A7%D9%86%D9%87_%DA%A9%D9%88%D8%B1%D9%88%D8%B4_-_cite_note-15

[10] https://fa.wikipedia.org/wiki/%D8%A7%D8%B3%D8%AA%D9%88%D8%A7%D9%86%D9%87_%DA%A9%D9%88%D8%B1%D9%88%D8%B4_-_cite_note-16

[11] https://fa.wikipedia.org/wiki/%D8%A7%DB%8C%D8%A7%D9%84%D8%A7%D8%AA_%D9%85%D8%AA%D8%AA

که در سال ۱۹۷۱ میلادی، پاول ریچارد برگر با بررسی متن آن متوجه شد که این قطعهٔ کوچک مربوط به بخشی از استوانهٔ کوروش است و از آن پس، این قطعه به‌صورت امانت در موزهٔ بریتانیا نگهداری می‌شود.[12]

متن حاوی روایتی از فتح بابل توسط کوروش در ۵۳۹ پ. م. است و با گفتاری از مردوخ[13] ایزد بابلی در مورد جنایت‌های نبونعید،[14] آخرین پادشاه کلدانی، آغاز می‌شود (سطرهای ۴ ۸). در ادامه روایتی از جستجوی مردوخ[15] برای یافتن پادشاه شایسته، انتساب کوروش به حکمرانی تمام جهان و عاملیت او در فتح بابل بدون جنگ آورده می‌شود (سطرهای ۹ ۱۹). سپس کوروش، با لحن اول شخص، القاب و نسب خود را برمی‌شمرد (سطرهای ۲۰ ۲۲) و اعلام می‌کند که صلح کشور را تضمین‌کرده (سطرهای ۲۲ ۲۶) که به موجب آن او و پسرش کمبوجیه مشمول رحمت مردوخ شده‌اند (سطرهای ۲۶ ۳۰). او بازسازی معبد، که در دوران زمامداری نبونعید به فراموشی سپرده شده بود و اجازه‌اش به تبعیدشدگان مبنی بر بازگشت به میهن‌شان را توصیف می‌کند (سطرهای ۳۰ ۳۶). در پایان، پادشاه بازسازی دفاع شهر بابل را توصیف کرده (سطرهای ۳۶ ۴۳) و گزارش می‌کند که به هنگام بازسازی، کتیبه‌ای از

%AA%D8%AD%D8%AF%D9%87_%D8%A2%D9%85%D8%B1%DB%8C%DA%A9%D8%A7

[12] https://fa.wikipedia.org/wiki/%D8%A7%D8%B3%D8%AA%D9%88%D8%A7%D9%86%D9%87_%DA%A9%D9%88%D8%B1%D9%88%D8%B4_-_cite_note-17

[13] https://fa.wikipedia.org/wiki/%D9%85%D8%B1%D8%AF%D9%88%D8%AE

[14] https://fa.wikipedia.org/wiki/%D9%86%D8%A8%D9%88%D9%86%D8%B9%DB%8C%D8%AF

[15] https://fa.wikipedia.org/wiki/%D9%85%D8%B1%D8%AF%D9%88%D8%AE

آشوربانیپال[16] را دید. (سطرهای ۴۳ ۴۵)[17]

ترجمهٔ استوانهٔ کوروش[18]

۱) [آن هنگام که مر]دوک، پادشاه همهٔ آسمان و زمین، [.......، ... (که) در ...ِیش [...ِ دشمنانش (؟) را] ویران می‌کند.

۲) [.................................] با دانایی گسترده (؟)، [... که گو]شه‌های جهان [را نظاره (؟) می‌کند]،

۳) ....بزر]گزاده اش (=ِیلشَزَر)، فرومایه‌ای به سروری سرزمینش گمارده شد.

۴) [...] .... (نبوئید) [فرمانروایی (؟) سا]ختگی بر آنان گمارد،

۵) نمونه‌ای (ساختگی) از اِسَگیل سا]خت و ....] برای (شهر) اور و دیگر جایگاه‌های مقدس [........]

---

[16] https://fa.wikipedia.org/wiki/%D8%A2%D8%B4%D9%88%D8%B1%D8%A8%D8%A7%D9%86%DB%8C%E2%80%8C%D9%BE%D8%A7%D9%84

[17] https://fa.wikipedia.org/wiki/%D8%A7%D8%B3%D8%AA%D9%88%D8%A7%D9%86%D9%87_%DA%A9%D9%88%D8%B1%D9%88%D8%B4_-_cite_note-18

[18] https://fa.wikipedia.org/w/index.php?title=%D8%A7%D8%B3%D8%AA%D9%88%D8%A7%D9%86%D9%87_%DA%A9%D9%88%D8%B1%D9%88%D8%B4&action=edit&section=5

۶) آیین‌هایی که شایستهٔ آنان (خدایان/پرستشگاه‌ها) نبود. پیشکشی[هایی ناپاک] .... بی پروا [...] هر روز یاوه سرایی می‌کرد و (به شیوه‌ای) [اها]نت آمیز

۷) پیشکشی‌های روزانه را بازداشت. او در [آیین‌ها دست برد و] .... درون پرستشگاه‌ها برقرار [کرد]. در دلش به ترس از مردوک شاه خدایان پایان [داد].

۸) هر روز به شهرش (=شهر مردوک) بدی روا می‌داشت [...] .... همهٔ مردما[ن]ش (=مردمان مردوک) را با یوغی رها نشدنی به نابودی کشاند.

۹) اِنلیل خدایان (=مردوک)، از شِکوهٔ ایشان بسیار خشمگین شد، و [.............] قلمرو آنان (را ؟) ....]. خدایانی که درون آنها می‌زیستند محراب هایشان را رها کردند،

۱۰) خشمگین از اینکه او (=نبونئید) (آنان را) (=خدایان غیر بابلی) به (شهر) شوآنّهَ (=بابل) وارد کرده بود. مردوکِ بلند[پایه، انلیلِ خدایان] برحم آمد. (او) به همهٔ زیستگاه‌هایی که جایگاه‌های (مقدس) شان ویران گشته بود

۱۱) و مردم سرزمین سومر و آکد که همچون کالبد مردگان شده بودند، اندیشه[اش] را بگردانید (و) بر آنان رحم آورد. او همهٔ سرزمین‌ها را جست و بررسی کرد،

۱۲) شاهی دادگر را جستجو کرد که دلخواهش باشد. او کورش، شاه (شهر) انشان را به دستانش گرفت و او را به نام خواند، (و) شهریاری او را بر همگان به آوای بلند

بَرخواند.

۱۳) او (=مردوک) سرزمین گوتی (و) همهٔ سپاهیان مادی را در برابر پاهای او (=کورش) به کرنش درآورد و همهٔ مردمان سرسیاه (=عامهٔ مردم) را که (مردوک) به دستان او (=کورش) سپرده بود،

۱۴) به دادگری و راستی شبانی کرد. مردوک، سرور بزرگ، که پرورندهٔ مردمانش است، به کارهای نیک او (=کورش) و دل راستینش به شادی نگریست

۱۵) (و) او را فرمان داد تا بسوی شهرش (=شهر مردوک)، بابل، برود. او را واداشت (تا) راه (شهر) تینتیر (=بابل) را در پیش گیرد و همچون دوست و همراهی در کنارش گام برداشت.

۱۶) سپاهیان گستردهٔ اش که شمارشان همچون آب یک رودخانه شمردنی نبود، پوشیده در جنگ‌افزارهایشان در کنارش روان بودند.

۱۷) (مردوک) او (=کورش) را بدون جنگ و نبرد، به درون (شهر) شوآنّهَ (=بابل) وارد کرد (و) شهرش، بابل را از سختی رهانید. او (=مردوک) نبونئید، شاهی را که از او نمی‌هراسید، در دستش (=دست کورش) نهاد.

۱۸) همهٔ مردم بابل، تمامی سرزمین سومر و آکد، بزرگان و فرمانبرداران در برابرش کرنش کردند (و) بر پاهایش بوسه زدند، از پادشاهی او شادمان گشتند (و) چهره هایشان درخشان شد.

۱۹) آنان (مردوک)، سروری را که با یاری اش به مردگان

زندگی بخشید (و) آنکه همه را از سختی و دشواری رهانید، شادمانه ستایش کردند و نامش را ستودند.

۲۰) منم کورش، شاه جهان، شاه بزرگ، شاه نیرومند، شاه بابل، شاه سومر و آکد، شاه چهارگوشهٔ جهان.

۲۱) پسر کمبوجیه، شاه بزرگ، شاه شهر انشان، نوهٔ کورش، شاه بزرگ، شا[ه شهر] انشان، نوادهٔ چیش پیش، شاه بزرگ، شاه شهر انشان،

۲۲) دودمان جاودانهٔ پادشاهی، که خدایان بِل و نَبو فرمانرواییش را دوست می‌دارند (و) پاد[شا]هی او را با دلی شاد یاد می‌کنند. آنگاه که با آشتی به در[ون] بابل در آمدم،

۲۳) جایگاه سروری (خود) را با جشن و شادمانی در کاخ شاهی برپا کردم. مردوک، سرور بزرگ، قلب گشادهٔ کسی که بابل را دوست دارد، همچون سرنوشتم به من [بخشید] (و) من هر روز ترسان در پی نیایش اش بودم.

۲۴) سپاهیان گسترده‌ام با آرامش درون بابل گام برمی داشتند. نگذاشتم کسی در همهٔ [سومر و] آکد هراس آفرین باشد.

۲۵) در پی امنیت ⸢شهر⸣ بابل و همهٔ جایگاه‌های مقدسش بودم. برای مردم بابل [...........] که بر خلاف خوا[ست خدایان] یوغی بر آنان نهاده بود که شایسته شان نبود،

۲۶) خستگی هایشان را تسکین دادم (و) از بندها (؟) رهایشان کردم. مردوک، سرور بزرگ، از رفتار [نیک من]

شادمان گشت (و)

۲۷) به من کورش، شاهی که از او می‌ترسد و کمبوجیه پسر تنی‌[ام و به] همهٔ سپاهیانم،

۲۸) برکتی نیکو ارزانی داشت، تا با آرامش، شادمانه در حضورش باشیم. به [فرمان] والایش، همهٔ شاهانی که بر تخت‌ها نشسته‌اند،

۲۹) از هر گوشهٔ (جهان)، از دریای بالا تا دریای پایین، آنانکه در [سرزمین‌های دور دست] می‌زیند، (و) شاهان سرزمین آموررّو که در چادرها زندگی می‌کنند، همهٔ آنان،

۳۰) باج سنگینشان را به بابل آوردند و بر پاهایم بوسه زدند. از [شوآنّه] (=بابل) تا شهر آشور و شوش،

۳۱) آکد، سرزمین اِشنونه، شهر زَمبَن، شهر مِتورنو، دِر، تا مرز گوتی، جایگاه[های مقدس آنسو]ی دجله که از دیرباز محراب هایشان ویران شده بود،

۳۲) خدایانی را که درون آنها ساکن بودند، به جایگاه هایشان بازگرداندم و (آنان را) در جایگاه‌های ابدی خودشان نهادم. همهٔ مردمانِ آنان (=آن خدایان) را گرد آوردم و به سکونتگاه هایشان بازگرداندم

۳۳) و خدایانِ سرزمین سومر و آکد را که نبونئید در میان خشم سرور خدایان به بابل آورده بود، به فرمان مردوک، سرور بزرگ، به سلامت

۳۴) به جایگاه هایشان بازگرداندم، جایگاهی که دلشادشان می‌سازد. باشد تا همهٔ خدایانی که به درون نیایشگاه

هایشان بازگرداندم،

۳۵) هر روز در برابر (خدایان) بِل و نَبو، روزگاری دراز (=عمری طولانی) برایم خواستار شوند (و) کارهای نیکم را یادآور شوند و به مردوک، سرورم، چنین گویند که "کورش، شاهی که از تو می‌هراسد و کمبوجیه پسرش

۳۶) ... [... (باشد که) آنان تا روزگاران دراز(؟)، سهمیه دهندگان نیایشگاه‌هایمان باشند" و (؟)] (باشد که) مردمان بابل شاهی مرا ⌐بستایندم. من همهٔ سرزمین‌ها را در صلح (امنیت) نشاندم.

۳۷) .... [غا]ز، دو مرغابی و ده کبوتر، بیشتر از [پیشکشی پیشین] غازها و مرغابی‌ها و کبوترهایی که

۳۸) .... [روزا]نه افزودم. در پی استوار کردن باروی دیوار ایمگور انلیل، دیوار بزرگ بابل برآمدم

۳۹) [....................................] دیواری از آجر پخته، بر کنارهٔ خندقی که شاهی پیشین ساخته بود، ولی سا[ختش را به پایان نبرده بود] ... کار آن را [... به پایان بردم.]

۴۰) ... که [شهر را] از بیرون [در بر نگرفته بود]، که (هیچ) شاهی پیش از من (با) کارگرانِ به بیگاری [گرفته شدهٔ سرزمینش در] بابل نساخته بود.

۴۱) [....................................] (آن را) [با قیر] و آجر پخته از نو برپا کردم و [ساختش را به پایان رساندم].

۴۲) [..................................] دروازه‌های بزرگ از چوب‌های سِدر] با روکش مفرغین. من همهٔ آن درها را با آستانه [ها و قطعات مسی] کار گذاردم.

۴۳) [..................................] کتیبه‌ای از] آشوربانیپال، شاهی پیش از من، [(بر آن) نو]شته شده بود، [درون آن دید]م.

۴۴) [..................................] در جای خود [نهادم (؟)] .... (باشد که) مردوک، سرور بزرگ، همچون هدیه‌ای به من عطا کند زندگانی دراز، [(و) عمری کامل،]

۴۵) [تختی ایمن و سلطنتی پایدار، و باشد که من .... در قلبت تا به] جاوان

Writing Found on the Cylinder of Cyrus

1. [When ... Mar]duk, king of the whole of heaven and earth, the .... who, in his ..., lays waste his.......
2. [..]
broad? in intelligence, ... who inspects (?) the world quarters (regions)
3. [...]his [first]born (=Belshazzar), a low person, was put in charge of his country,
4. but [...] he set [a (...) counter]feit over them.
5. He ma[de] a counterfeit of Esagil, [and ....]... for Ur and the rest of the cult-cities.

6. Rites inappropriate to them, [impure] fo[od-offerings..]disrespectful [...] were daily gabbled, and, as an insult,
7. he brought the daily offerings to a halt; he inter[fered with the rites and] instituted [.......] within the sanctuaries. In his mind, reverential fear of Marduk, king of the gods, came to an end.
8. He did yet more evil to his city every day; ... his [people ....], he brought ruin on them all by a yoke without relief.
9. Enlil-of-the-gods became extremely angry at their complaints, and [...] their territory. The gods who lived within them left their shrines,
10. angry that he had made (them) enter into Shuanna (Babylon). Ex[alted Marduk, Enlil-of-the-Go]ds, relented. He changed his mind about all the settlements whose sanctuaries were in ruins,
11. and the population of the land of Sumer and Akkad who had become like corpses, and took pity on them. He inspected and checked all the countries,
12. seeking for the upright king of his choice. He took the hand of Cyrus, king of the city of Anshan, and called him by his name, proclaiming him aloud for the kingship over all of everything.
13. He made the land of Guti and all the Median troops prostrate themselves at his feet, while he shepherded in justice and righteousness the black-headed people

14. whom he had put under his care. Marduk, the great lord, who nurtures his people, saw with pleasure his fine deeds and true heart,
15. and ordered that he should go to Babylon. He had him take the road to Tintir (Babylon), and, like a friend and companion, he walked at his side.
16. His vast troops whose number, like the water in a river, could not be counted, were marching fully-armed at his side.
17. He had him enter without fighting or battle right into Shuanna; he saved his city Babylon from hardship. He handed over to him Nabonidus, the king who did not fear him.
18. All the people of Tintir, of all Sumer and Akkad, nobles and governors, bowed down before him and kissed his feet, rejoicing over his kingship and their faces shone.
19. The lord through whose help all were rescued from death and who saved them all from distress and hardship, they blessed him sweetly and praised his name.
20. I am Cyrus, king of the universe, the great king, the powerful king, king of Babylon, king of Sumer and Akkad, king of the four quarters of the world,
21. son of Cambyses, the great king, king of the city of Anshan, grandson of Cyrus, the great king, ki[ng of the ci]ty of Anshan, descendant of Teispes, the great king, king of the city of Anshan,
22. the perpetual seed of kingship, whose reign Bel (Marduk)and Nabu love, and with whose kingship, to their joy, they concern themselves.

When I went as harbinger of peace i[nt]o Babylon

23. I founded my sovereign residence within the palace amid celebration and rejoicing. Marduk, the great lord, bestowed on me as my destiny the great magnanimity of one who loves Babylon, and I every day sought him out in awe.
24. My vast troops were marching peaceably in Babylon, and the whole of [Sumer] and Akkad had nothing to fear.
25. I sought the safety of the city of Babylon and all its sanctuaries. As for the population of Babylon [..., w]ho as if without div[ine intention] had endured a yoke not decreed for them,
26. I soothed their weariness; I freed them from their bonds(?). Marduk, the great lord, rejoiced at [my good] deeds,
27. and he pronounced a sweet blessing over me, Cyrus, the king who fears him, and over Cambyses, the son [my] issue, [and over] my all my troops,
28. that we might live happily in his presence, in well-being. At his exalted command, all kings who sit on thrones,
29. from every quarter, from the Upper Sea to the Lower Sea, those who inhabit [remote distric]ts (and) the kings of the land of Amurru who live in tents, all of them,
30. brought their weighty tribute into Shuanna, and kissed my feet. From [Shuanna] I sent back to their places to the city of Ashur and Susa,

31. Akkad, the land of Eshnunna, the city of Zamban, the city of Meturnu, Der, as far as the border of the land of Guti - the sanctuaries across the river Tigris - whose shrines had earlier become dilapidated,
32. the gods who lived therein, and made permanent sanctuaries for them. I collected together all of their people and returned them to their settlements,
33. and the gods of the land of Sumer and Akkad which Nabonidus –to the fury of the lord of the gods – had brought into Shuanna, at the command of Marduk, the great lord,
34. I returned them unharmed to their cells, in the sanctuaries that make them happy. May all the gods that I returned to their sanctuaries,
35. every day before Bel and Nabu, ask for a long life for me, and mention my good deeds, and say to Marduk, my lord, this: "Cyrus, the king who fears you, and Cambyses his son,
36. may they be the provisioners of our shrines until distant (?) days, and the population of Babylon call blessings on my kingship. I have enabled all the lands to live in peace."
37. Every day I increased by [… ge]ese, two ducks and ten pigeons the [former offerings] of geese, ducks and pigeons.
38. I strove to strengthen the defences of the wall Imgur-Enlil, the great wall of Babylon,
39. and [I completed] the quay of baked brick on the bank of the moat which an earlier king had bu[ilt but not com]pleted its work.
40. [I …… which did not surround the city] outside, which no earlier king had built, his

workforce, the levee [from his land, in/int]o Shuanna.

41. [..with bitum]en and baked brick I built anew, and [completed] its [work].
42. [...]great [doors of cedar wood] with bronze cladding,
43. [and I installed] all their doors, threshold slabs and door fittings with copper parts. [.......................]. I saw within it an inscription of Ashurbanipal, a king who preceded me;
44. [...] in its place. May Marduk, the great lord, present to me as a gift a long life and the fullness of age,
45. [a secure throne and an enduring rei]gn, [and may I …... in] your heart forever.

a. [Written and check]ed [from a…]; (this) tablet (is) of
b. Qishti-Marduk, son of […].

CHAPTER 13
EXCERPTS FROM THE GOSPELS

انجیل متی فصل 5

موعظهٔ سر کوه

1وقتی عیسی جمعیّت زیادی را دید، به بالای کوهی رفت و در آنجا نشست و شاگردانش به نزد او آمدند 2و او دهان خود را گشوده به آنان چنین تعلیم داد:

خوشبختی واقعی

(لوقا 6:20 23)

«3خوشا به حال کسانی‌که از فقر روحی خود آگاهند

زیرا، پادشاهی آسمان از آن ایشان است.

«4خوشا به حال ماتم‌زدگان،

زیرا ایشان تسلّی خواهند یافت.

«5خوشا به حال فروتنان،

زیرا ایشان مالک جهان خواهند شد.

«6خوشا به حال کسانی‌که گرسنه و تشنهٔ نیکی خدایی هستند،

زیرا ایشان سیر خواهند شد.

«7خوشا به حال رحم‌کنندگان،

زیرا ایشان رحمت را خواهند دید.

«8خوشا به حال پاکدلان،

زیرا ایشان خدا را خواهند دید.

«9خوشا به حال صلح‌کنندگان،

زیرا ایشان فرزندان خدا خوانده خواهند شد.

«10خوشا به حال کسانی‌که در راه نیکی آزار می‌بینند،

زیرا پادشاهی آسمان از آن ایشان است.

11«خوشحال باشید اگر بخاطر من به شما اهانت می‌کنند و آزار می‌رسانند و به ناحق هرگونه افترایی به شما می‌زنند.12خوشحال باشید و بسیار شادی کنید، زیرا پاداش شما در آسمان عظیم است، چون همین‌طور به انبیای قبل از شما نیز آزار می‌رسانیدند.

نمک و نور

(مرقس 9:50 لوقا 34:14 35)

13«شما نمک جهان هستید ولی هرگاه نمک مزهٔ خود را از دست بدهد، چگونه می‌توان آن را بار دیگر نمکین ساخت؟ دیگر مصرفی ندارد، جز آنکه بیرون ریخته پایمال مردم شود.

14«شما نور جهان هستید. نمی‌توان شهری را که بر کوهی بنا

شده است، پنهان کرد. 15هیچ‌کس چراغ روشن نمی‌کند که آن را زیر سرپوش بگذارد، بلکه آن را بر چراغ‌پایه قرار می‌دهد تا به تمام ساکنان خانه نور دهد. 16نور شما نیز باید همین‌طور در برابر مردم بتابد تا کارهای نیک شما را ببینند و پدر آسمانی شما را ستایش نمایند.

شریعت

17«فکر نکنید که من آمده‌ام تا تورات و نوشته‌های انبیا را منسوخ نمایم. نیامده‌ام تا منسوخ کنم، بلکه تا به کمال برسانم. 18یقین بدانید که تا آسمان و زمین بر جای هستند، هیچ حرف و نقطه‌ای از تورات از بین نخواهد رفت تا همهٔ آن به انجام برسد. 19پس هرگاه کسی حتّی کوچکترین احکام شریعت را بشکند و به دیگران چنین تعلیم دهد در پادشاهی آسمان پست‌ترین فرد محسوب خواهد شد. حال آنکه هرکس شریعت را نگاه دارد و به دیگران نیز چنین تعلیم دهد، در پادشاهی آسمان بزرگ خوانده خواهد شد. 20بدانید که تا نیکی شما از نیکی علما و فریسیان بیشتر نباشد، به پادشاهی آسمان وارد نخواهید شد.

خشم و غضب

21«شنیده‌اید که در قدیم به مردم گفته شد: 'قتل نکن و هرکس مرتکب قتل شود محکوم خواهد شد.' 22امّا من به شما می‌گویم: هرکس نسبت به برادر خود عصبانی شود، محکوم خواهد شد و

هرکه برادر خود را ابلَه بخواند، به دادگاه برده خواهد شد و اگر او را 'احمق' بخواند مستوجب آتش جهنم خواهد بود. 23پس اگر هدیۀ خود را به قربانگاه ببری و در آنجا به‌خاطر بیاوری که برادرت از تو شکایتی دارد، 24هدیۀ خود را جلوی قربانگاه بگذار و اول برو با برادر خود آشتی کن و آنگاه برگرد و هدیۀ خویش را تقدیم کن.

25«با مدّعی خود وقتی‌که هنوز در راه دادگاه هستی صلح نما وگرنه آن مدّعی تو را به دست قاضی خواهد سپرد و قاضی تو را به دست زندانبان خواهد داد و به زندان خواهی افتاد. 26یقین بدان که تا ریال آخر را نپردازی، آزاد نخواهی شد.

زِنا

27«شنیده‌اید که گفته شده: 'زنا نکن' 28امّا من به شما می‌گویم هرگاه مردی از روی شهوت به زنی نگاه کند در دل خود با او زنا کرده است. 29پس اگر چشم راست تو باعث گمراهی تو می‌شود، آن را بیرون آور و دورانداز؛ زیرا بهتر است که عضوی از بدن خود را از دست بدهی تا اینکه با تمام بدن به جهنم افکنده شوی. 30اگر دست راستت تو را گمراه می‌سازد، آن را ببر و دور انداز؛ زیرا بهتر است که عضوی از بدن خود را از دست بدهی تا اینکه با تمام بدن به جهنم بیفتی.

طلاق

(متی 19:9، مرقس 11:10 و 12، لوقا 18:16)

31«همچنین گفته شده: 'هرگاه مردی زن خود را طلاق دهد، باید طلاقنامه‌ای به او بدهد.' 32امّا من به شما می‌گویم: هرگاه کسی زن خود را جز به علّت زنا طلاق دهد، او را به زناکاری می‌کشاند و هرکس با چنین زنی ازدواج نماید، زنا می‌کند.

سوگند خوردن

33«همچنین شنیده‌اید که در قدیم به مردم گفته شده: 'قسم دروغ نخور و به هر سوگندی که به نام خداوند یاد کرده‌ای عمل نما.' 34امّا من می‌گویم به هیچ وجه قسم یاد نکن، نه به آسمان زیرا که عرش خداست، 35نه به زمین زیرا که پای‌انداز اوست، نه به اورشلیم زیرا که شهر آن پادشاه بزرگ است 36و نه به سر خود، زیرا قادر نیستی مویی از آن را سیاه یا سفید کنی. 37سخن شما فقط بلی یا خیر باشد. زیاده بر این از شیطان است.

انتقام

(لاویان 29:6 30)

38«شنیده‌اید که گفته شده: 'چشم به عوض چشم و دندان به عوض دندان.' 39امّا من به شما می‌گویم به کسی‌که به تو بدی می‌کند بدی نکن و اگر کسی بر گونهٔ راست تو سیلی می‌زند، گونهٔ دیگر خود را به طرف او بگردان. 40هرگاه کسی تو را برای گرفتن پیراهنت به دادگاه بکشاند، کت خود را هم به او ببخش. 41هرگاه شخصی تو را به پیمودن یک کیلومتر راه مجبور

نماید دو کیلومتر با او برو. 42به کسی‌که از تو چیزی می‌خواهد ببخش و از کسی‌که تقاضای قرض می‌کند، روی نگردان.

مهربانی با دشمن

(لوقا 27:6، 28، 32، 36)

43«شنیده‌اید که: 'همسایه‌ات را دوست بدار و با دشمن خویش دشمنی کن.' 44امّا من به شما می‌گویم دشمنان خود را دوست بدارید و برای کسانی‌که به شما آزار می‌رسانند دعا کنید. 45به این وسیله شما فرزندان پدر آسمانی خود خواهید شد، چون او آفتاب خود را بر بدان و نیکان، یکسان می‌تاباند و باران خود را بر درستکاران و بدکاران می‌باراند. 46اگر فقط کسانی را دوست بدارید که شما را دوست دارند، چه اجری دارید؟ مگر باجگیران همین کار را نمی‌کنند؟ 47اگر فقط به دوستان خود سلام کنید چه کار فوق‌العاده‌ای کرده‌اید؟ مگر بی‌دینان همین کار را نمی‌کنند؟ 48پس شما باید کامل باشید همان‌طور که پدر آسمانی شما کامل است.

خشم و غضب

»21شنیده‌اید که در قدیم به مردم گفته شد: 'قتل نکن و هرکس مرتکب قتل شود محکوم خواهد شد22'. امّا من به شما می‌گویم: هرکس نسبت به برادر خود عصبانی شود، محکوم خواهد شد و

هرکه برادر خود را ابلَه بخواند، به دادگاه برده خواهد شد و اگر او را 'احمق' بخواند مستوجب آتش جهنم خواهد بود.23 پس اگر هدیۀ خود را به قربانگاه ببری و در آنجا بهخاطر بیاوری که برادرت از تو شکایتی دارد، 24هدیۀ خود را جلوی قربانگاه بگذار و اول برو با برادر خود آشتی کن و آنگاه برگرد و هدیۀ خویش را تقدیم کن.

«25با مدّعی خود وقتیکه هنوز در راه دادگاه هستی صلح نما وگرنه آن مدّعی تو را به دست قاضی خواهد سپرد و قاضی تو را به دست زندانبان خواهد داد و به زندان خواهی افتاد.26 یقین بدان که تا ریال آخر را نپردازی، آزاد نخواهی شد.

زنا

«27شنیدهاید که گفته شده: 'زنا نکن'.28 امّا من به شما میگویم هرگاه مردی از روی شهوت به زنی نگاه کند در دل خود با او زنا کرده است.29 پس اگر چشم راست تو باعث گمراهی تو میشود، آن را بیرون آور و دور انداز؛ زیرا بهتر است که عضوی از بدن خود را از دست بدهی تا اینکه با تمام بدن به جهنم افکنده شوی.30 اگر دست راستت تو را گمراه میسازد، آن را ببر و دور انداز؛ زیرا بهتر است که عضوی از بدن خود را از دست بدهی تا اینکه با تمام بدن به جهنم بیفتی.

طلاق

(متی 19:9، مرقس 11:10، 12، لوقا 16 : 18)

«31همچنین گفته شده: 'هرگاه مردی زن خود را طلاق دهد، باید طلاق‌نامه‌ای به او بدهد32.' امّا من به شما می‌گویم: هرگاه کسی زن خود را جز به علّت زنا طلاق دهد، او را به زناکاری می‌کشاند و هرکس با چنین زنی ازدواج نماید، زنا می‌کند.

سوگند خوردن

«33همچنین شنیده‌اید که در قدیم به مردم گفته شده: 'قسم دروغ نخور و به هر سوگندی که به نام خداوند یاد کرده‌ای عمل نما34.' امّا من می‌گویم به هیچ وجه قسم یاد نکن، نه به آسمان زیرا که عرش خداست، 35نه به زمین زیرا که پای‌انداز اوست، نه به اورشلیم زیرا که شهر آن پادشاه بزرگ است 36و نه به سر خود، زیرا قادر نیستی مویی از آن را سیاه یا سفید کنی37. سخن شما فقط بلی یا خیر باشد. زیاده بر این از شیطان است.

انتقام

(لاویا 29:6 30)

«38شنیده‌اید که گفته شده: 'چشم به عوض چشم و دندان به عوض دندان39.' امّا من به شما می‌گویم به کسی‌که به تو بدی می‌کند بدی نکن و اگر کسی بر گونهٔ راست تو سیلی می‌زند، گونهٔ دیگر خود را به طرف او بگردان40. هرگاه کسی تو را برای گرفتن پیراهنت به دادگاه بکشاند، کت خود را هم به او ببخش41. هرگاه شخصی تو را به پیمودن یک کیلومتر راه مجبور

نماید دو کیلومتر با او برو42. به کسی‌که از تو چیزی می‌خواهد ببخش و از کسی‌که تقاضای قرض می‌کند، روی نگردان.

مهربانی با دشمن
(لوقا 27:6 , 28 , 32 , 36)

»43شنیده‌اید که: 'همسایه‌ات را دوست بدار و با دشمن خویش دشمنی کن'44. امّا من به شما می‌گویم دشمنان خود را دوست بدارید و برای کسانی‌که به شما آزار می‌رسانند دعا کنید45. به این وسیله شما فرزندان پدر آسمانی خود خواهید شد، چون او آفتاب خود را بر بدان و نیکان، یکسان می‌تاباند و باران خود را بر درستکاران و بدکاران می‌باراند46. اگر فقط کسانی را دوست بدارید که شما را دوست دارند، چه اجری دارید؟ مگر باجگیران همین کار را نمی‌کنند؟ 47اگر فقط به دوستان خود سلام کنید چه کار فوق‌العاده‌ای کرده‌اید؟ مگر بی‌دینان همین کار را نمی‌کنند؟ 48پس شما باید کامل باشید همان‌طور که پدر آسمانی شما کامل است.

متی فصل 6
صدقه دادن

»1مواظب باشید که وظایف دینی خود را برای جلب توجّه مردم

در انظار دیگران انجام ندهید زیرا اگر چنین کنید، هیچ اجری نزد پدر آسمانی خود ندارید.

»2پس هرگاه صدقه می‌دهی آن را با ساز و کرنا اعلام نکن، چنانکه ریاکاران در کنیسه‌ها و خیابانها می‌کنند تا مورد ستایش مردم قرار بگیرند. یقین بدانید که آنان اجر خود را یافته‌اند3 !و امّا تو، هرگاه صدقه می‌دهی، نگذار دست چپ تو از آنچه دست راستت می‌کند آگاه شود4. از صدقه دادن تو کسی باخبر نشود و پدری که هیچ چیز از نظر او پنهان نیست، اجر تو را خواهد داد.

دعا

(لوقا 11:2 4)

»5وقتی دعا می‌کنید مانند ریاکاران نباشید. آنان دوست دارند در کنیسه‌ها و گوشه‌های خیابانها بایستند و دعا بخوانند تا مردم آنان را ببینند. یقین بدانید که آنها اجر خود را یافته‌اند6! هرگاه تو دعا می‌کنی به اندرون خانهٔ خود برو، در را ببند و در خلوت، در حضور پدر نادیدهٔ خود دعا کن و پدری که هیچ چیز از نظر او پنهان نیست، اجر تو را خواهد داد7. در وقت دعا مانند بت‌پرستان وِردهای بی‌معنی را تکرار نکنید، آنان گمان می‌کنند با تکرار زیاد، دعایشان مستجاب می‌شود8. پس مثل ایشان نباشید زیرا پدر شما احتیاجات شما را پیش از آنکه از او بخواهید می‌داند9. پس شما این‌طور دعا کنید:

"ای پدر آسمانی ما،

نام تو مقدّس باد.

10پادشاهی تو بیاید.

ارادهٔ تو همان‌طور که در آسمان اجرا می‌شود، در زمین نیز اجرا شود.

11نان روزانهٔ ما را امروز به ما بده.

12خطاهای ما را ببخش،

چنانکه ما نیز خطاکاران خود را می‌بخشیم.

13ما را در وسوسه‌ها میاور بلکه ما را از شریر رهایی ده،

زیرا پادشاهی و قدرت و جلال تا ابدالآباد از آن توست.

آمین'.

»14چون اگر شما خطاهای دیگران را ببخشید پدر آسمانی شما نیز شما را خواهد بخشید15. امّا اگر شما مردم را نبخشید پدر آسمانی شما نیز خطاهای شما را نخواهد بخشید.

روزه

»16وقتی روزه می‌گیرید مانند ریاکاران، خودتان را پریشان نشان ندهید. آنان قیافه‌های خود را تغییر می‌دهند تا روزه‌دار بودن خود را به رُخ دیگران بکشند. یقین بدانید که آنها اجر خود را یافته‌اند17! امّا تو وقتی روزه می‌گیری، سر خود را شانه کُن و صورت خود را بشوی 18تا مردم از روزهٔ تو باخبر نشوند، بلکه

فقط پدر تو که در نهان است، آن را بداند و پدری که هیچ چیز از نظر او پنهان نیست، اجر تو را خواهد داد.

گنجِ آسمانی

(لوقا 12:33 34)

»19گنجهای خود را بر روی زمین، جایی‌که بید و زنگ به آن زیان می‌رساند و دزدان نقب زده آن را می‌دزدند، ذخیره نکنید.20بلکه گنجهای خود را در عالَم بالا، یعنی در جایی‌که بید و زنگ به آن آسیبی نمی‌رسانند و دزدان نقب نمی‌زنند و آن را نمی‌دزدند، ذخیره کنید.21 زیرا هرجا گنج توست، دل تو نیز در آنجا خواهد بود.

چراغِ بدن

(لوقا 11:34 36)

»22چراغ بدن، چشم است. اگر چشم تو سالم باشد، تمام وجودت روشن است 23امّا اگر چشم تو سالم نباشد تمام وجودت در تاریکی خواهد بود. پس اگر آن نوری که در توست تاریک باشد، آن، چه تاریکی عظیمی خواهد بود!

خدا و دارایی

(لوقا 16:13، 12:22 31)

»24هیچ‌کس نمی‌تواند بندهٔ دو ارباب باشد، چون یا از اولی بدش می‌آید و دومی را دوست دارد و یا به اولی ارادت پیدا می‌کند

و دومی را حقیر می‌شمارد. شما نمی‌توانید هم بندهٔ خدا باشید و هم در بند مال.

»25بنابراین به شما می‌گویم: برای زندگی خود نگران نباشید، که چه بخورید و یا چه بیاشامید و نه برای بدن خود که چه بپوشید، زیرا زندگی از غذا و بدن از لباس مهمتر است 26. به پرندگان نگاه کنید: آنها نه می‌کارند، نه درو می‌کنند و نه در انبارها ذخیره می‌کنند، ولی پدر آسمانی شما روزیِ آنها را می‌دهد. مگر ارزش شما به مراتب از آنها بیشتر نیست؟ 27کدامیک از شما می‌تواند با نگرانی ساعتی به عمر خود بیافزاید؟

»28چرا برای لباس نگران هستید؟ به سوسن‌های صحرا نگاه کنید و ببینید چگونه نمو می‌کنند، آنها نه زحمت می‌کشند و نه می‌ریسند 29. ولی بدانید که حتّی سلیمان هم با آن‌همه حشمت و جلالش مثل یکی از آنها آراسته نشد 30. پس اگر خدا علف صحرا را که امروز هست و فردا در تنور ریخته می‌شود این‌طور می‌آراید، آیا شما را، ای کم‌ایمانان، بمراتب بهتر نخواهد پوشانید!

»31پس نگران نباشید و نگویید: 'چه بخوریم؟ چه بنوشیم؟' و یا چه بپوشیم؟' 32'تمام ملل جهان برای به دست آوردن این چیزها تلاش می‌کنند، امّا پدر آسمانی شما می‌داند که شما به همهٔ این چیزها احتیاج دارید 33. شما قبل از هر چیز برای به دست آوردن پادشاهی خدا و انجام خواسته‌های او بکوشید، آن وقت همهٔ این

چیز ها نیز به شما داده خواهد شد34. پس نگران فردا نباشید، نگرانی فردا برای فرداست و بدی امروز برای امروز کافی است.

متی فصل 7

قضاوت دربارۀ دیگران

(لوقا 37:6 ,38 , 41 42)

»1دربارۀ دیگران قضاوت نکنید تا مورد قضاوت قرار نگیرید2. همان‌طور که شما دیگران را محکوم می‌کنید خودتان نیز محکوم خواهید شد. با هر پیمانه‌ای که به دیگران بدهید، با همان پیمانه عوض خواهید گرفت3. چرا پر کاهی را که در چشم برادرت هست می‌بینی، ولی در فکر چوب بزرگی که در چشم خود داری نیستی؟ 4یا چگونه جرأت می‌کنی به برادر خود بگویی: 'اجازه بده پر کاه را از چشمت بیرون آورم' حال آنکه خودت چوب بزرگی در چشم داری5. ای ریاکار، اول آن چوب بزرگ را از چشم خود بیرون بیاور، آنگاه درست خواهی دید که پر کاه را از چشم برادرت بیرون بیاوری6. آنچه مقدّس است به سگان ندهید و مرواریدهای خود را جلوی خوکها نریزید. مبادا آنها را زیر پا لگدمال کنند و برگشته شما را بَدَرَند.

خواستن، جستجو کردن و کوبیدن

(لوقا 9:11 13)

»7بخواهید، به شما داده خواهد شد. بجویید، پیدا خواهید کرد. در بزنید، در به رویتان باز خواهد شد8. چون هرکه بخواهد، به دست می‌آورد و هرکه بجوید، پیدا می‌کند و هرکه در بزند، در به رویش باز می‌شود9. آیا کسی در میان شما هست که وقتی پسرش از او نان بخواهد، سنگی به او بدهد؟ 10و یا وقتی ماهی می‌خواهد، ماری در دستش بگذارد؟ 11پس اگر شما که انسانهای شریری هستید، می‌دانید چگونه باید چیزهای خوب را به فرزندان خود بدهید، چقدر بیشتر باید مطمئن باشید که پدر آسمانی شما چیزهای نیکو را به آنانی که از او تقاضا می‌کنند عطا خواهد فرمود12 ابا دیگران همان‌طور رفتار کنید که می‌خواهید آنها با شما رفتار کنند. این است خلاصهٔ تورات و نوشته‌های انبیا.

درِ تنگ

(لوقا 24:13)

»13از در تنگ وارد شوید، زیرا دری که بزرگ و راهی که وسیع است به هلاکت منتهی می‌شود و کسانی‌که این راه را می‌پیمایند، بسیارند 14امّا دری که به حیات منتهی می‌شود تنگ و راهش دشوار است و یابندگان آن هم، کم هستند.

درخت و میوهٔ آن

(لوقا 43:6 44)

»15از انبیای دروغین برحذر باشید که در لباس میش به نزد

شما می‌آیند، ولی در باطن گرگان درّنده‌اند۱۶. آنان را از کارهایشان خواهید شناخت. آیا می‌توان از بوتهٔ خار، انگور و از خاربن، انجیر چید؟ ۱۷همین‌طور درخت خوب میوهٔ خوب به بار می‌آورد و درخت فاسد میوهٔ بد۱۸. درخت خوب نمی‌تواند میوهٔ بد به بار آورد و نه درخت بد میوهٔ خوب۱۹. درختی که میوهٔ خوب به بار نیاورد آن را می‌برند و در آتش می‌اندازند۲۰. بنابراین شما آنها را از میوه‌هایشان خواهید شناخت.

شما را نمی‌شناسم

(لوقا ۱۳:۲۵ ۲۷)

»۲۱نه هرکس که مرا «خداوندا، خداوندا» خطاب کند به پادشاهی آسمان وارد خواهد شد، بلکه کسی‌که ارادهٔ پدر آسمانی مرا به انجام برساند۲۲. وقتی آن روز برسد بسیاری به من خواهند گفت: 'خداوندا، خداوندا، آیا به نام تو نبوّت نکردیم؟ آیا با ذکر نام تو دیوها را بیرون نراندیم؟ و به نام تو معجزات بسیار نکردیم؟ ۲۳آنگاه آشکارا به آنان خواهم گفت: 'من هرگز شما را نشناختم. از من دور شوید، ای بدکاران'.

دو خانه

(لوقا ۶:۴۷ ۴۹)

»۲۴پس کسی‌که سخنان مرا می‌شنود و به آنها عمل می‌کند، مانند شخص دانایی است که خانهٔ خود را بر سنگ بنا

نمود25. باران بارید، سیل جاری شد و باد وزیده بر آن خانه فشار آورد، امّا آن خانه خراب نشد زیرا شالودهٔ آن بر روی سنگ بود.

26«امّا هرکه سخنان مرا بشنود و به آنها عمل نکند مانند شخص نادانی است که خانهٔ خود را بر روی شن بنا کرد27. باران بارید، سیل جاری شد و باد وزیده به آن خانه فشار آورد و آن خانه فرو ریخت و چه خرابی عظیمی بود»!

28وقتی عیسی این سخنان را به پایان رسانید مردم از تعالیم او متحیّر شدند 29زیرا او برخلاف روش علما، با اختیار و اقتدار به آنان تعلیم می‌داد.

Matthew Chapters 5-7, of the Gospels (NKJV)

1 And seeing the multitudes, He went up on a mountain, and when He was seated His disciples came to Him. 2 Then He opened His mouth and taught them, saying: 3 "Blessed [are] the poor in spirit, For theirs is the kingdom of heaven. 4 Blessed [are] those who mourn, For they shall be comforted. 5 Blessed [are] the meek, For they shall inherit the earth. 6 Blessed [are] those who hunger and thirst for righteousness, For they shall be filled. 7 Blessed [are] the merciful, For they shall obtain mercy. 8 Blessed [are] the pure in heart, For they shall see God. 9 Blessed [are] the peacemakers, For they shall be called sons of God. 10 Blessed [are] those who are persecuted for righteousness' sake, For theirs is the kingdom of heaven. 11 "Blessed are you when they revile and persecute you, and say all kinds of evil

against you falsely for My sake. 12 "Rejoice and be exceedingly glad, for great [is] your reward in heaven, for so they persecuted the prophets who were before you. 13 "You are the salt of the earth; but if the salt loses its flavor, how shall it be seasoned? It is then good for nothing but to be thrown out and trampled underfoot by men. 14 "You are the light of the world. A city that is set on a hill cannot be hidden. 15 "Nor do they light a lamp and put it under a basket, but on a lampstand, and it gives light to all [who are] in the house. 16 "Let your light so shine before men, that they may see your good works and glorify your Father in heaven. 17 "Do not think that I came to destroy the Law or the Prophets. I did not come to destroy but to fulfill. 18 "For assuredly, I say to you, till heaven and earth pass away, one jot or one tittle will by no means pass from the law till all is fulfilled. 19 "Whoever therefore breaks one of the least of these commandments, and teaches men so, shall be called least in the kingdom of heaven; but whoever does and teaches [them], he shall be called great in the kingdom of heaven. 20 "For I say to you, that unless your righteousness exceeds [the righteousness] of the scribes and Pharisees, you will by no means enter the kingdom of heaven. 21 "You have heard that it was said to those of old, 'You shall not murder, and whoever murders will be in danger of the judgment.' 22 "But I say to you that whoever is angry with his brother without a cause shall be in danger of the judgment. And whoever says to his brother, 'Raca!' shall be in danger of the council. But whoever says, 'You fool!' shall be in danger of Gehenna fire. 23 "Therefore if you bring your gift to the altar, and there remember that your brother has something against you, 24 "leave your gift there before the altar, and go your way. First be reconciled to your brother, and then come and offer your gift. 25 "Agree with your adversary quickly, while you are on the way with him, lest your adversary deliver you to the judge, the judge hand you over to the officer, and you be thrown into prison. 26 "Assuredly, I say to you, you will by no means get out of there till you have paid the last penny. 27 "You have heard that it was said to those of old, 'You shall not commit adultery.' 28 "But I say to you that whoever looks at a woman to lust for her has already committed adultery with her in his heart. 29 "If your right eye causes you to sin, pluck it out and cast [it] from you; for it is more profitable for you that one of your members perish, than for your whole body to be cast into Gehenna. 30 "And if your right hand causes you to sin, cut it off and cast [it] from you; for it is more profitable for you that one of your members perish, than for your whole body to be cast into Gehenna. 31 "Furthermore it has been said, 'Whoever divorces his wife, let him give her a certificate of divorce.' 32 "But I say to you that whoever divorces his wife for any reason except sexual immorality causes her to commit adultery; and whoever marries a woman who is divorced commits adultery. 33 "Again you have heard that it was said to those of old, 'You shall not swear falsely, but shall perform your oaths to the Lord.' 34 "But I say to you, do not swear at all: neither by heaven, for it is God's throne; 35 "nor by the earth, for it is His footstool; nor by Jerusalem, for it is the city of the great King. 36 "Nor shall you swear by your head, because you cannot make one hair white or black. 37 "But let your 'Yes' be 'Yes,' and your 'No,' 'No.' For whatever is more than these is from the evil one. 38 "You have heard that it was said, 'An eye for an eye and a tooth for a tooth.' 39 "But I tell you not to resist an evil person. But whoever slaps you on your right cheek, turn the other to him also. 40 "If anyone wants to sue you and take away your tunic, let him have [your] cloak also. 41 "And whoever compels you to go one mile, go with him two. 42 "Give to him who asks you, and from him who wants to borrow from you do not turn away. 43 "You have heard that it was said, 'You shall love your neighbor and hate your enemy.' 44 "But I say to you, love your enemies, bless those who curse you, do good to those who hate you, and pray for those who spitefully use you and persecute you, 45 "that you may be sons of your Father in heaven; for He makes His sun rise on the evil and on the good, and sends rain on the just and on the unjust. 46 "For if you love those who love you, what reward have you? Do not even the tax collectors do the same? 47 "And if you greet your brethren only, what do you do more [than others]? Do not even the tax collectors do so? 48 "Therefore you shall be perfect, just as your Father in heaven is perfect.

6:1 "Take heed that you do not do your charitable deeds before men, to be seen by them. Otherwise you have no reward from your Father in heaven. 2 "Therefore, when you do a charitable deed, do not sound a trumpet before you as the hypocrites do in the synagogues and in the streets, that they may have glory from men. Assuredly, I say to you, they have their reward. 3 "But when you do a charitable deed, do not let your left hand know what your right hand is doing, 4 "that your charitable deed may be in secret;

and your Father who sees in secret will Himself reward you openly. 5 "And when you pray, you shall not be like the hypocrites. For they love to pray standing in the synagogues and on the corners of the streets, that they may be seen by men. Assuredly, I say to you, they have their reward. 6 "But you, when you pray, go into your room, and when you have shut your door, pray to your Father who [is] in the secret [place]; and your Father who sees in secret will reward you openly. 7 "And when you pray, do not use vain repetitions as the heathen [do]. For they think that they will be heard for their many words. 8 "Therefore do not be like them. For your Father knows the things you have need of before you ask Him. 9 "In this manner, therefore, pray: Our Father in heaven, Hallowed be Your name. 10 Your kingdom come. Your will be done On earth as [it is] in heaven. 11 Give us this day our daily bread. 12 And forgive us our debts, As we forgive our debtors. 13 And do not lead us into temptation, But deliver us from the evil one. For Yours is the kingdom and the power and the glory forever. Amen. 14 "For if you forgive men their trespasses, your heavenly Father will also forgive you. 15 "But if you do not forgive men their trespasses, neither will your Father forgive your trespasses. 16 "Moreover, when you fast, do not be like the hypocrites, with a sad countenance. For they disfigure their faces that they may appear to men to be fasting. Assuredly, I say to you, they have their reward. 17 "But you, when you fast, anoint your head and wash your face, 18 "so that you do not appear to men to be fasting, but to your Father who [is] in the secret [place]; and your Father who sees in secret will reward you openly. 19 "Do not lay up for yourselves treasures on earth, where moth and rust destroy and where thieves break in and steal; 20 "but lay up for yourselves treasures in heaven, where neither moth nor rust destroys and where thieves do not break in and steal. 21 "For where your treasure is, there your heart will be also. 22 "The lamp of the body is the eye. If therefore your eye is good, your whole body will be full of light. 23 "But if your eye is bad, your whole body will be full of darkness. If therefore the light that is in you is darkness, how great [is] that darkness! 24 "No one can serve two masters; for either he will hate the one and love the other, or else he will be loyal to the one and despise the other. You cannot serve God and mammon. 25 "Therefore I say to you, do not worry about your life, what you will eat or what you will drink; nor about your body, what you will put on. Is not life more than food and the body more than clothing? 26 "Look at the birds of the air, for they neither sow nor reap nor gather into barns; yet your heavenly Father feeds them. Are you not of more value than they? 27 "Which of you by worrying can add one cubit to his stature? 28 "So why do you worry about clothing? Consider the lilies of the field, how they grow: they neither toil nor spin; 29 "and yet I say to you that even Solomon in all his glory was not arrayed like one of these. 30 "Now if God so clothes the grass of the field, which today is, and tomorrow is thrown into the oven, [will He] not much more [clothe] you, O you of little faith? 31 "Therefore do not worry, saying, 'What shall we eat?' or 'What shall we drink?' or 'What shall we wear?' 32 "For after all these things the Gentiles seek. For your heavenly Father knows that you need all these things. 33 "But seek first the kingdom of God and His righteousness, and all these things shall be added to you. 34 "Therefore do not worry about tomorrow, for tomorrow will worry about its own things. Sufficient for the day [is] its own trouble.

7:1 "Judge not, that you be not judged. 2 "For with what judgment you judge, you will be judged; and with the measure you use, it will be measured back to you. 3 "And why do you look at the speck in your brother's eye, but do not consider the plank in your own eye? 4 "Or how can you say to your brother, 'Let me remove the speck from your eye'; and look, a plank [is] in your own eye? 5 "Hypocrite! First remove the plank from your own eye, and then you will see clearly to remove the speck from your brother's eye. 6 "Do not give what is holy to the dogs; nor cast your pearls before swine, lest they trample them under their feet, and turn and tear you in pieces. 7 "Ask, and it will be given to you; seek, and you will find; knock, and it will be opened to you. 8 "For everyone who asks receives, and he who seeks finds, and to him who knocks it will be opened. 9 "Or what man is there among you who, if his son asks for bread, will give him a stone? 10 "Or if he asks for a fish, will he give him a serpent? 11 "If you then, being evil, know how to give good gifts to your children, how much more will your Father who is in heaven give good things to those who ask Him! 12 "Therefore, whatever you want men to do to you, do also to them, for this is the Law and the Prophets. 13 "Enter by the narrow gate; for wide [is] the gate and broad [is] the way that leads to destruction, and there are many who go in by it. 14 "Because narrow [is] the gate and difficult [is] the way which leads to life, and there are few who find it. 15 "Beware of false prophets, who come to you in sheep's clothing, but inwardly they are ravenous wolves. 16 "You will know them by their fruits. Do men gather grapes from thornbushes or figs from thistles? 17 "Even so, every good tree bears good fruit, but a bad tree bears bad fruit. 18 "A good tree cannot bear bad fruit, nor [can] a bad tree bear good fruit. 19 "Every tree that does not bear good fruit is cut down and thrown into the fire. 20 "Therefore by their fruits you will know them. 21 "Not everyone who says to Me, 'Lord, Lord,' shall enter the kingdom of heaven, but he who does the will of My Father in heaven. 22 "Many will say to Me in that day, 'Lord, Lord, have we not prophesied in Your name, cast out demons in Your name, and done many wonders in Your name?' 23 "And then I will declare to them, 'I never knew you; depart from Me, you who practice lawlessness!' 24 "Therefore whoever hears these sayings of Mine, and does them, I will liken him to a wise man who built his house on the rock: 25 "and the rain descended, the floods came, and the winds blew and beat on that house; and it did not fall, for it was founded on the rock. 26 "But everyone who hears these sayings of Mine, and does not do them, will be like a foolish man who built his house on the sand: 27 "and the rain descended, the floods came, and the winds blew and beat on that house; and it fell. And great was its fall." 28 And so it was, when Jesus had ended these sayings, that the people were astonished at His teaching, 29 for He taught them as one having authority, and not as the scribes.

انجیل یوحنا فصل 1

کلمهٔ حیات

1در ازل کلمه بود. کلمه با خدا بود و کلمه خود خدا بود، 2از ازل کلمه با خدا بود 3. همه چیز به وسیلهٔ او هستی یافت و بدون او چیزی آفریده نشد 4. حیات از او به وجود آمد و آن حیات 5نور آدمیان بود. نور در تاریکی می‌تابد و تاریکی هرگز بر آن چیره نشده است.

6مردی به نام یحیی ظاهر شد که فرستادهٔ خدا بود 7. او آمد تا شاهد باشد و بر آن نور شهادت دهد تا به وسیلهٔ او همه ایمان بیاورند 8. او خود آن نور نبود، بلکه آمد تا بر آن نور شهادت دهد 9. آن نور واقعی که همهٔ آدمیان را نورانی می‌کند، در حال آمدن بود.

10او در جهان بود و جهان به وسیلهٔ او آفریده شد، امّا جهان او را نشناخت 11. او به قلمرو خود آمد ولی متعلّقانش او را قبول نکردند 12. امّا به همهٔ کسانی‌که او را قبول کردند و به او ایمان آوردند، این امتیاز را داد که فرزندان خدا شوند 13که نه مانند تولّدهای معمولی و نه در اثر تمایلات نفسانی یک پدر جسمانی، بلکه از خدا تولّد یافتند.

14کلمه انسان شد و در میان ما ساکن گردید. ما شکوه و جلالش را دیدیم، شکوه و جلالی شایستهٔ فرزند یگانهٔ پدر و پر از فیض و

راستی.

15شهادت یحیی این بود که فریاد می‌زد و می‌گفت: «این همان شخصی است که دربارهٔ او گفتم که بعد از من می‌آید امّا بر من برتری و تقدّم دارد، زیرا پیش از تولّد من، او وجود داشت».

16از فیض سرشار او، پیوسته برکات فراوانی یافته‌ایم17. زیرا شریعت به وسیلهٔ موسی عطا شد، امّا فیض و راستی توسط عیسی مسیح آمد18. کسی هرگز خدا را ندیده است، امّا آن فرزند یگانه‌ای که در ذات پدر و از همه به او نزدیکتر است او را شناسانیده است.

پیام یحیای تعمیددهنده

(متی 1:3 12، مرقس 1:1 8، لوقا 1:3 18)

19این است شهادت یحیی وقتی یهودیان اورشلیم، کاهنان و لاویان را نزد او فرستادند تا بپرسند که او کیست.

20او از جواب دادن خودداری نکرد، بلکه به طور واضح اعتراف نموده گفت: «من مسیح نیستم».

21آنها از او پرسیدند «پس آیا تو الیاس هستی؟» پاسخ داد: «خیر.» آنها پرسیدند: «آیا تو آن نبی موعود هستی؟» پاسخ داد: «خیر».

22پرسیدند: «پس تو کیستی؟ ما باید به فرستندگان خود جواب بدهیم، دربارهٔ خودت چه می‌گویی؟» 23«او از زبان اشعیای نبی پاسخ داده گفت: «من صدای ندا کننده‌ای هستم که در بیابان فریاد

می‌زند، 'راه خداوند را راست گردانید'».

24این قاصدان که از طرف فریسیان فرستاده شده بودند 25از او پرسیدند: «اگر تو نه مسیح هستی و نه الیاس و نه آن نبی موعود، پس چرا تعمید می‌دهی؟»

26یحیی پاسخ داد: «من با آب تعمید می‌دهم، امّا کسی در میان شما ایستاده است که شما او را نمی‌شناسید27. او بعد از من می‌آید، ولی من حتّی شایستهٔ آن نیستم که بند کفشهایش را باز کنم».

28این ماجرا در بیت‌عنیا، یعنی آن طرف رود اردن، در جایی‌که یحیی مردم را تعمید می‌داد، واقع شد.

برّهٔ خدا

29روز بعد، وقتی یحیی عیسی را دید که به طرف او می‌آید، گفت: «نگاه کنید این است آن برّهٔ خدا که گناه جهان را برمی‌دارد30. این است آن کسی‌که درباره‌اش گفتم که بعد از من مردی می‌آید که بر من تقدّم و برتری دارد، زیرا پیش از تولّد من او وجود داشته است31. من او را نمی‌شناختم، امّا آمدم تا با آب تعمید دهم و به این وسیله او را به اسرائیل بشناسانم».

32یحیی شهادت خود را این‌طور ادامه داد: «من روح خدا را دیدم که به صورت کبوتری از آسمان آمد و بر او قرار گرفت33. من او را نمی‌شناختم امّا آن کسی‌که مرا فرستاد تا با آب تعمید دهم به من گفته بود، هرگاه ببینی که روح بر کسی نازل شود

و بر او قرار گیرد، بدان که او همان کسی است که به روح‌القدس تعمید می‌دهد. 34. من این را دیده‌ام و شهادت می‌دهم که او پسر خداست.»

اولین شاگردان عیسی

35 روز بعد هم یحیی با دو نفر از شاگردان خود ایستاده بود، 36 وقتی عیسی را دید که از آنجا می‌گذرد گفت: «این است برّهٔ خدا.»

37 آن دو شاگرد این سخن را شنیدند و به دنبال عیسی به راه افتادند. 38 عیسی برگشت و آن دو نفر را دید که به دنبال او می‌آیند. از آنها پرسید: «به دنبال چه می‌گردید؟» آنها گفتند: «ربی (یعنی ای استاد) منزل تو کجاست؟»

39 او به ایشان گفت: «بیایید و ببینید.» پس آن دو نفر رفتند و دیدند کجا منزل دارد و بقیّهٔ روز را نزد او ماندند. زیرا تقریباً ساعت چهار بعد از ظهر بود.

40 یکی از آن دو نفر، که بعد از شنیدن سخنان یحیی به دنبال عیسی رفت، اندریاس برادر شمعون پطرس بود. 41 او اول برادر خود شمعون را پیدا کرد و به او گفت: «ما ماشیح (یعنی مسیح) را یافته‌ایم.» 42 پس وقتی اندریاس، شمعون را نزد عیسی برد، عیسی به شمعون نگاه کرد و گفت: «تویی شمعون پسر یونا، ولی بعد از این کیفا (یا پطرس به معنی صخره) نامیده می‌شوی.»

فیلیپُس و نتنائیل

43روز بعد، وقتی عیسی می‌خواست به جلیل برود، فیلیپُس را یافته به او گفت: «به دنبال من بیا» 44.فیلیپُس مانند اندریاس و پطرس اهل بیت‌صیدا بود 45.فیلیپُس هم رفت و نتنائیل را پیدا کرد و به او گفت: «ما آن کسی را که موسی در تورات ذکر کرده و انبیا دربارهٔ او سخن گفته‌اند، پیدا کرده‌ایم او عیسی پسر یوسف و از اهالی ناصره است».

46نتنائیل به او گفت: «آیا می‌شود که از ناصره چیز خوبی بیرون بیاید؟» فیلیپُس جواب داد: «بیا و ببین».

47وقتی عیسی نتنائیل را دید که به طرف او می‌آید گفت: «این است یک اسرائیلی واقعی که در او هیچ مکری وجود ندارد».

48نتنائیل پرسید: «مرا از کجا می‌شناسی؟» عیسی جواب داد: «پیش از آنکه فیلیپُس تو را صدا کند، وقتی زیر درخت انجیر بودی، من تو را دیدم».

49نتنائیل گفت: «ای استاد، تو پسر خدا هستی! تو پادشاه اسرائیل می‌باشی»!

50عیسی در جواب گفت: «آیا فقط به علّت اینکه به تو گفتم تو را زیر درخت انجیر دیدم ایمان آوردی؟ بعد از این کارهای بزرگتری خواهی دید 51.آنگاه به او گفت: «یقین بدانید که شما آسمان را گشوده و فرشتگان خدا را در حالی‌که بر پسر انسان

صعود و نزول می‌کنند خواهید دید».

John Chapter 1, of the Gospels (NKJV)

1 In the beginning was the Word, and the Word was with God, and the Word was God. 2 He was in the beginning with God. 3 All things were made through Him, and without Him nothing was made that was made. 4 In Him was life, and the life was the light of men. 5 And the light shines in the darkness, and the darkness did not comprehend it. 6 There was a man sent from God, whose name [was] John. 7 This man came for a witness, to bear witness of the Light, that all through him might believe. 8 He was not that Light, but [was sent] to bear witness of that Light. 9 That was the true Light which gives light to every man coming into the world. 10 He was in the world, and the world was made through Him, and the world did not know Him. 11 He came to His own, and His own did not receive Him. 12 But as many as received Him, to them He gave the right to become children of God, to those who believe in His name: 13 who were born, not of blood, nor of the will of the flesh, nor of the will of man, but of God. 14 And the Word became flesh and dwelt among us, and we beheld His glory, the glory as of the only begotten of the Father, full of grace and truth. 15 John bore witness of Him and cried out, saying, "This was He of whom I said, 'He who comes after me is preferred before me, for He was before me.' " 16 And of His fullness we have all received, and grace for grace. 17 For the law was given through Moses, [but] grace and truth came through Jesus Christ. 18 No one has seen God at any time. The only begotten Son, who is in the bosom of

the Father, He has declared [Him]. 19 Now this is the testimony of John, when the Jews sent priests and Levites from Jerusalem to ask him, "Who are you?" 20 He confessed, and did not deny, but confessed, "I am not the Christ." 21 And they asked him, "What then? Are you Elijah?" He said, "I am not." "Are you the Prophet?" And he answered, "No." 22 Then they said to him, "Who are you, that we may give an answer to those who sent us? What do you say about yourself?" 23 He said: "I [am] 'The voice of one crying in the wilderness: "Make straight the way of the LORD," ' as the prophet Isaiah said." 24 Now those who were sent were from the Pharisees. 25 And they asked him, saying, "Why then do you baptize if you are not the Christ, nor Elijah, nor the Prophet?" 26 John answered them, saying, "I baptize with water, but there stands One among you whom you do not know. 27 "It is He who, coming after me, is preferred before me, whose sandal strap I am not worthy to loose." 28 These things were done in Bethabara beyond the Jordan, where John was baptizing. 29 The next day John saw Jesus coming toward him, and said, "Behold! The Lamb of God who takes away the sin of the world! 30 "This is He of whom I said, 'After me comes a Man who is preferred before me, for He was before me.' 31 "I did not know Him; but that He should be revealed to Israel, therefore I came baptizing with water." 32 And John bore witness, saying, "I saw the Spirit descending from heaven like a dove, and He remained upon Him. 33 "I did not know Him, but He who sent me to baptize with water said to me, 'Upon whom you see the Spirit descending, and remaining on Him, this is He who baptizes with the Holy Spirit.' 34 "And I have seen and testified that this is the Son of God." 35 Again, the next day, John stood with two of his disciples. 36 And looking at Jesus as He walked, he said, "Behold the Lamb of God!" 37 The two disciples heard him speak, and they followed Jesus. 38 Then Jesus turned, and seeing them following, said to them, "What do you seek?" They said to Him, "Rabbi" (which is to say, when translated, Teacher), "where are You staying?" 39 He said to them, "Come and see." They came and saw where He was staying, and remained with Him that day (now it was about the tenth hour). 40 One of the two who heard John [speak], and followed Him, was Andrew, Simon Peter's brother. 41 He first found his own brother Simon, and said to him, "We have found the Messiah" (which is translated, the Christ). 42 And he brought him to Jesus. Now when Jesus looked at him, He said, "You are Simon the son of Jonah. You shall be called Cephas" (which is translated, A Stone). 43 The following day Jesus wanted to go to Galilee, and He found Philip and said to him, "Follow Me." 44 Now Philip was from Bethsaida, the city of Andrew and Peter. 45 Philip found Nathanael and said to him, "We have found Him of whom Moses in the law, and also the prophets, wrote--Jesus of Nazareth, the son of Joseph." 46 And Nathanael said to him, "Can anything good come out of Nazareth?" Philip said to him, "Come and see." 47 Jesus saw Nathanael coming toward Him, and said of him, "Behold, an Israelite indeed, in whom is no deceit!" 48 Nathanael said to Him, "How do You know me?" Jesus answered and said to him, "Before Philip called you, when you were under the fig tree, I saw you." 49 Nathanael answered and said to Him, "Rabbi, You are the Son of God! You are the King of Israel!" 50 Jesus answered and said to him, "Because I said to you, 'I saw you under the fig tree,' do you believe? You will see greater things than these." 51 And He said to him, "Most assuredly, I say to you, hereafter you shall see heaven open, and the angels of God ascending and descending upon the Son of Man."

انجیل مرقس فصل 1

یحیای تعمیددهنده

(متی 3:1، 12، لوقا 3:1، 18، یوحنا 1:28 19)

1ابتدای انجیل عیسی مسیح پسر خدا 2: در کتاب اشعیای نبی آمده است که:

«من قاصد خود را پیشاپیش تو می‌فرستم،

او راه تو را باز خواهد کرد.

3ندا کننده‌ای در بیابان فریاد می‌زند:

راه خداوند را آماده سازید و

مسیر او را راست گردانید.»

4یحیای تعمید دهنده در بیابان ظاهر شد و اعلام کرد که مردم برای آمرزش گناهان، باید توبه کنند و تعمید بگیرند 5. مردم از تمام سرزمین یهودیه و شهر اورشلیم نزد او می‌رفتند و با اعتراف به گناهان خود، در رود اردن به وسیلۀ او تعمید می‌گرفتند 6. لباس یحیی از پشم شتر بود و کمربندی چرمی به کمر می‌بست و

خوراکش ملخ و عسل صحرایی بود7. او اعلام کرده گفت: «بعد از من مردی تواناتر از من می‌آید که من لایق آن نیستم که خم شوم و بند کفشهایش را باز کنم8. من شما را با آب تعمید می‌دهم، امّا او شما را با روح‌القدس تعمید خواهد داد.»

تعمید و آزمایش عیسی

(متی 13:3، 11:4، لوقا 21:3 22، 1:4 13)

9در این هنگام عیسی از ناصرهٔ جلیل آمد و در رود اردن از یحیی تعمید گرفت10. همینکه عیسی از آب بیرون آمد، دید که آسمان شکافته شد و روح‌القدس به صورت کبوتری به سوی او فرود آمد11. و آوازی از آسمان شنیده شد که می‌گفت: «تو پسر عزیز من هستی، از تو خشنودم12.» فوراً روح خدا او را به بیابان برد13. او مدّت چهل روز در بیابان بود و شیطان او را وسوسه می‌کرد. عیسی در بین حیوانات وحشی بود و فرشتگان او را خدمت می‌کردند.

دعوت چهار ماهیگیر

(متی 12:4 22، 14:4 15، لوقا 1:5 11)

14پس از بازداشت یحیی، عیسی به استان جلیل آمد و مژدهٔ خدا را اعلام فرمود 15و گفت: «ساعت مقرّر رسیده و پادشاهی خدا نزدیک است. توبه کنید و به این مژده ایمان آورید16.» وقتی عیسی در کنار دریاچهٔ جلیل قدم می‌زد، شمعون و برادرش

اندریاس را دید که تور به دریا می‌انداختند چون ماهیگیر بودند17. عیسی به آنها فرمود: «دنبال من بیایید تا شما را صیّاد مردم گردانم»18. آن دو نفر فوراً تورهایشان را گذاشته، به دنبال او رفتند19. کمی دورتر عیسی، یعقوب پسر زِبدی و برادرش یوحنا را دید که در قایقی مشغول آماده کردن تورهای خود بودند20. عیسی آن دو نفر را نیز فوراً نزد خود خواند. آنها پدر خود زِبدی را با کارگرانش در قایق ترک کردند و به دنبال او رفتند.

شفای مرد دیوانه

(لوقا 4:31 37)

21عیسی و شاگردانش وارد کفرناحوم شدند و همینکه روز سبت فرا رسید، عیسی به کنیسه رفت و به تعلیم پرداخت22. مردم از طرز تعلیم او حیران ماندند، زیرا برخلاف علمای یهود، او با اقتدار و اختیار به آنها تعلیم می‌داد23. در همان موقع مردی که روح پلید داشت، وارد کنیسه شد و فریاد زد24: «ای عیسای ناصری با ما چه‌کار داری؟ آیا آمده‌ای تا ما را نابود کنی؟ من می‌دانم تو کیستی، ای قدّوس خدا»25. امّا عیسی او را سرزنش کرده گفت: «ساکت شو و از این مرد بیرون بیا»26. روح پلید آن مرد را تکان سختی داد و با فریاد بلند از او خارج شد27. همه چنان حیران شدند، که از یکدیگر می‌پرسیدند: «این چیست؟ چه

تعالیم تازه‌ای است و با چه قدرتی به ارواح پلید فرمان می‌دهد و آنها اطاعت می‌کنند»!

28بزودی شهرت او در سراسر جلیل پیچید.

شفای دردمندان

(متی 8:14، 17، لوقا 4:38 41)

29عیسی و شاگردانش از کنیسه بیرون آمدند و به اتّفاق یعقوب و یوحنا یکراست به خانهٔ شمعون و اندریاس رفتند. 30مادر زن شمعون تب داشت و خوابیده بود. به محض اینکه عیسی به آنجا رسید او را از حال آن زن باخبر کردند. 31عیسی نزد او رفت، دستش را گرفت و او را برخیزانید، تبش قطع شد و به پذیرایی آنها پرداخت.

32وقتی خورشید غروب کرد و شب شد، همهٔ بیماران و دیوانگان را نزد او آوردند. 33تمام مردم شهر در جلوی آن خانه جمع شدند. 34عیسی بیماران بسیاری را که امراض گوناگون داشتند، شفا داد و دیوهای زیادی را بیرون کرد و نگذاشت آنها حرفی بزنند، چون او را می‌شناختند.

موعظه در جلیل

(لوقا 4:42 44)

35سحرگاه روز بعد، عیسی از خواب برخاسته از منزل خارج شد و به جای خلوتی رفت و مشغول دعا شد. 36شمعون و

همراهانش به جستجوی او پرداختند ۳۷. و وقتی او را پیدا کردند به او گفتند: «همه به دنبال تو می‌گردند».

۳۸عیسی به آنها فرمود: «به جاهای دیگر و شهرهای اطراف برویم تا در آنجا هم پیام خود را برسانم، چون من برای همین منظور آمده‌ام».

۳۹عیسی در سراسر جلیل می‌گشت و در کنیسه‌ها پیام خود را اعلام می‌کرد و دیوها را بیرون می‌نمود.

شفای جذامی

(متی ۸: ۱ لوقا ۵: ۱۲ ۱۶)

۴۰یک نفر جذامی نزد عیسی آمد، زانو زد و تقاضای کمک کرد و گفت: «اگر بخواهی می‌توانی مرا پاک سازی».

۴۱دل عیسی به حال او سوخت، دست خود را دراز کرد، او را لمس نمود و فرمود: «البتّه می‌خواهم، پاک شو» ۴۲. فوراً جذامش برطرف شد و پاک گشت ۴۳. بعد عیسی درحالی‌که او را مرخّص می‌کرد با تأکید فراوان ۴۴به او فرمود: «مواظب باش به کسی چیزی نگویی، بلکه برو خود را به کاهن نشان بده و به‌خاطر اینکه پاک شده‌ای قربانی‌ای را که موسی حکم کرده، تقدیم کن تا برای شفای تو شهادتی باشد».

۴۵امّا آن مرد رفت و این خبر را در همه‌جا منتشر کرد. به طوری که عیسی دیگر نمی‌توانست آشکارا وارد شهر بشود. بلکه

در جاهای خلوت شهر می‌ماند و مردم از همه طرف نزد او می‌رفتند.

Mark Chapter 1, of the Gospels (NKJV)

1 The beginning of the gospel of Jesus Christ, the Son of God. 2 As it is written in the Prophets: "Behold, I send My messenger before Your face, Who will prepare Your way before You." 3 "The voice of one crying in the wilderness: 'Prepare the way of the LORD; Make His paths straight.' " 4 John came baptizing in the wilderness and preaching a baptism of repentance for the remission of sins. 5 Then all the land of Judea, and those from Jerusalem, went out to him and were all baptized by him in the Jordan River, confessing their sins. 6 Now John was clothed with camel's hair and with a leather belt around his waist, and he ate locusts and wild honey. 7 And he preached, saying, "There comes One after me who is mightier than I, whose sandal strap I am not worthy to stoop down and loose. 8 "I indeed baptized you with water, but He will baptize you with the Holy Spirit." 9 It came to pass in those days [that] Jesus came from Nazareth of Galilee, and was baptized by John in the Jordan. 10 And immediately, coming up from the water, He saw the heavens parting and the Spirit descending upon Him like a dove. 11 Then a voice came from heaven, "You are My beloved Son, in whom I am well pleased." 12 Immediately the Spirit drove Him into the wilderness. 13 And He was there in the wilderness forty days, tempted by Satan, and was with the wild beasts; and the angels ministered to Him. 14 Now after John was put in prison, Jesus came

to Galilee, preaching the gospel of the kingdom of God, 15 and saying, "The time is fulfilled, and the kingdom of God is at hand. Repent, and believe in the gospel." 16 And as He walked by the Sea of Galilee, He saw Simon and Andrew his brother casting a net into the sea; for they were fishermen. 17 Then Jesus said to them, "Follow Me, and I will make you become fishers of men." 18 They immediately left their nets and followed Him. 19 When He had gone a little farther from there, He saw James the [son] of Zebedee, and John his brother, who also [were] in the boat mending their nets. 20 And immediately He called them, and they left their father Zebedee in the boat with the hired servants, and went after Him. 21 Then they went into Capernaum, and immediately on the Sabbath He entered the synagogue and taught. 22 And they were astonished at His teaching, for He taught them as one having authority, and not as the scribes. 23 Now there was a man in their synagogue with an unclean spirit. And he cried out, 24 saying, "Let [us] alone! What have we to do with You, Jesus of Nazareth? Did You come to destroy us? I know who You are--the Holy One of God!" 25 But Jesus rebuked him, saying, "Be quiet, and come out of him!" 26 And when the unclean spirit had convulsed him and cried out with a loud voice, he came out of him. 27 Then they were all amazed, so that they questioned among themselves, saying, "What is this? What new doctrine [is] this? For with authority He commands even the unclean spirits, and they obey Him." 28 And immediately His fame spread throughout all the region around Galilee. 29 Now as soon as they had come out of the synagogue, they entered the house of Simon and Andrew, with James and John. 30 But

Simon's wife's mother lay sick with a fever, and they told Him about her at once. 31 So He came and took her by the hand and lifted her up, and immediately the fever left her. And she served them. 32 At evening, when the sun had set, they brought to Him all who were sick and those who were demon-possessed. 33 And the whole city was gathered together at the door. 34 Then He healed many who were sick with various diseases, and cast out many demons; and He did not allow the demons to speak, because they knew Him. 35 Now in the morning, having risen a long while before daylight, He went out and departed to a solitary place; and there He prayed. 36 And Simon and those [who were] with Him searched for Him. 37 When they found Him, they said to Him, "Everyone is looking for You." 38 But He said to them, "Let us go into the next towns, that I may preach there also, because for this purpose I have come forth." 39 And He was preaching in their synagogues throughout all Galilee, and casting out demons. 40 Now a leper came to Him, imploring Him, kneeling down to Him and saying to Him, "If You are willing, You can make me clean." 41 Then Jesus, moved with compassion, stretched out [His] hand and touched him, and said to him, "I am willing; be cleansed." 42 As soon as He had spoken, immediately the leprosy left him, and he was cleansed. 43 And He strictly warned him and sent him away at once, 44 and said to him, "See that you say nothing to anyone; but go your way, show yourself to the priest, and offer for your cleansing those things which Moses commanded, as a testimony to them." 45 However, he went out and began to proclaim [it] freely, and to spread the matter, so that Jesus could no longer openly enter the city, but was outside in deserted places; and they came to Him from every direction.

انجیل لوقا فصل 1
گوسفند گمشده

(متی 14 12:18)

1در این هنگام باجگیران و خطاکاران ازدحام کرده بودند تا به سخنان او گوش دهند2. فریسیان و علما غرولندکنان گفتند: «این مرد اشخاص بی‌سروپا را با خوشرویی می‌پذیرد و با آنان غذا می‌خورد3 «.به این جهت عیسی مَثَلی آورد و گفت:

»4فرض کنید یکی از شما صد گوسفند داشته باشد و یکی از آنها را گُم کند، آیا نود و نُه تای دیگر را در چراگاه نمی‌گذارد و به دنبال آن گمشده نمی‌رود تا آن را پیدا کند؟ 5و وقتی آن را پیدا کرد با خوشحالی آن را به دوش می‌گیرد 6و به خانه می‌رود و همهٔ دوستان و همسایگان را جمع می‌کند و می‌گوید: 'با من شادی کنید، گوسفند گمشدهٔ خود را پیدا کرده‌ام7' 'بدانید که به همان طریق برای یک گناهکار که توبه می‌کند در آسمان بیشتر شادی و سرور خواهد بود تا برای نود و نه شخص پرهیزکار که نیازی به توبه ندارند.

سکّهٔ گمشده

»8و یا فرض کنید زنی ده سکهٔ نقره داشته باشد و یکی را گُم کند آیا چراغی روشن نمی‌کند و خانه را جارو نمی‌نماید و در هر گوشه به دنبال آن نمی‌گردد تا آن را پیدا کند؟ 9و وقتی پیدا کرد همهٔ دوستان و همسایگان خود را جمع می‌کند و می‌گوید: 'با من شادی کنید، سکه‌ای را که گُم کرده بودم، پیدا کردم10 '.به همان طریق بدانید که برای یک گناهکار که توبه می‌کند در میان فرشتگان خدا، شادی و سرور خواهد بود«.

پسر گمشده

11باز فرمود: »مردی بود که دو پسر داشت12 .پسر کوچکتر به پدر گفت: 'پدر، سهم مرا از دارایی خودت به من بده.' پس پدر دارایی خود را بین آن دو تقسیم کرد13 .چند روز بعد پسر کوچک تمام سهم خود را به پول نقد تبدیل کرد و رهسپار سرزمین دوردستی شد و در آنجا دارایی خود را در عیاشی به باد داد14 .وقتی تمام آن را خرج کرد قحطی سختی در آن سرزمین رخ داد و او سخت دچار تنگدستی شد15 .پس رفت و نوکر یکی از مَلّاکین آن محل شد. آن شخص او را به مزرعهٔ خود فرستاد تا خوکهایش را بچراند16 .او آرزو داشت شکم خود را با نواله‌هایی که خوکها می‌خورند پُر کند ولی هیچکس به او چیزی نمی‌داد17 .سرانجام به خود آمد و گفت: 'بسیاری از کارگران پدر من نان کافی و حتّی اضافی دارند و من در اینجا نزدیک است از

گرسنگی تلف شوم18. من برمی‌خیزم و نزد پدر خود می‌روم و به او می‌گویم: پدر، من نسبت به خدا و نسبت به تو گناه کرده‌ام19. دیگر لایق آن نیستم که پسر تو خوانده شوم. با من هم مثل یکی از نوکران خود رفتار کن20.' پس برخاست و رهسپار خانه پدر شد.

»هنوز تا خانه فاصلهٔ زیادی داشت که پدرش او را دید و دلش به حال او سوخت و به طرف او دوید، دست به گردنش انداخت و به گرمی او را بوسید21. پسر گفت: 'پدر، من نسبت به خدا و نسبت به تو گناه کرده‌ام. دیگر لایق آن نیستم که پسر تو خوانده شوم22.'. امّا پدر به نوکران خود گفت: 'زود بروید. بهترین ردا را بیاورید و به او بپوشانید. انگشتری به انگشتش و کفش به پاهایش کنید23. گوسالهٔ پرواری را بیاورید و سر ببرید تا مجلس جشنی برپا کنیم، 24چون این پسر من مرده بود، زنده شده و گُمشده بود، پیدا شده است.' به این ترتیب جشن و سرور شروع شد.

»25در این هنگام پسر بزرگتر در مزرعه بود و وقتی بازگشت، همینکه به خانه نزدیک شد صدای رقص و موسیقی را شنید26. یکی از نوکران را صدا کرد و پرسید: 'جریان چیست؟'27 نوکر به او گفت: 'برادرت آمده و پدرت چون او را صحیح و سالم باز یافته، گوسالهٔ پرواری را کشته است28.' امّا پسر بزرگ قهر کرد و به هیچ‌وجه نمی‌خواست به داخل بیاید

پدرش بیرون آمد و به او التماس نمود29. امّا او در جواب پدر گفت: 'تو خوب می‌دانی که من در این چند سال چطور مانند یک غلام به تو خدمت کرده‌ام و هیچ‌وقت از اوامر تو سرپیچی نکرده‌ام و تو حتّی یک بُزغاله هم به من نداده‌ای تا با دوستان خود خوش بگذرانم30. امّا حالا که این پسرت پیدا شده، بعد از آنکه همهٔ ثروت تو را با فاحشه‌ها تلف کرده است برای او گوسالهٔ پرواری می‌کُشی31 'پدر گفت: 'پسرم، تو همیشه با من هستی و هرچه من دارم مال توست32. امّا ما باید جشن بگیریم و شادی کنیم، زیرا این برادر توست که مرده بود، زنده شده است و گُمشده بود، پیدا شده است.»'

Luke Chapter 15, of the Gospels (NKJV)

1 Then all the tax collectors and the sinners drew near to Him to hear Him. 2 And the Pharisees and scribes complained, saying, "This Man receives sinners and eats with them." 3 So He spoke this parable to them, saying: 4 "What man of you, having a hundred sheep, if he loses one of them, does not leave the ninety-nine in the wilderness, and go after the one which is lost until he finds it? 5 "And when he has found [it], he lays [it] on his shoulders, rejoicing. 6 "And when he comes home, he calls together [his] friends and neighbors, saying to them, 'Rejoice with me, for I have found my sheep which was lost!' 7 "I say to you that likewise there will be more joy in heaven over one sinner who repents than over ninety-nine just persons who need no repentance. 8 "Or what woman, having

ten silver coins, if she loses one coin, does not light a lamp, sweep the house, and search carefully until she finds [it]? 9 "And when she has found [it], she calls [her] friends and neighbors together, saying, 'Rejoice with me, for I have found the piece which I lost!' 10 "Likewise, I say to you, there is joy in the presence of the angels of God over one sinner who repents." 11 Then He said: "A certain man had two sons. 12 "And the younger of them said to [his] father, 'Father, give me the portion of goods that falls [to me].' So he divided to them [his] livelihood. 13 "And not many days after, the younger son gathered all together, journeyed to a far country, and there wasted his possessions with prodigal living. 14 "But when he had spent all, there arose a severe famine in that land, and he began to be in want. 15 "Then he went and joined himself to a citizen of that country, and he sent him into his fields to feed swine. 16 "And he would gladly have filled his stomach with the pods that the swine ate, and no one gave him [anything]. 17 "But when he came to himself, he said, 'How many of my father's hired servants have bread enough and to spare, and I perish with hunger! 18 'I will arise and go to my father, and will say to him, "Father, I have sinned against heaven and before you, 19 "and I am no longer worthy to be called your son. Make me like one of your hired servants." ' 20 "And he arose and came to his father. But when he was still a great way off, his father saw him and had compassion, and ran and fell on his neck and kissed him. 21 "And the son said to him, 'Father, I have sinned against heaven and in your sight, and am no longer worthy to be called your son.' 22 "But the father said to his servants, 'Bring out the best robe and put [it] on him, and put a ring on his hand and sandals on [his] feet. 23 'And bring the fatted calf here and kill [it], and let us eat and be merry; 24 'for this my son was dead and is alive again; he was lost and is found.' And they began to be merry. 25 "Now his older son was in the field. And as he came and drew near to the house, he heard music and dancing. 26 "So he called one of the servants and asked what these things meant. 27 "And he said to him, 'Your brother has come, and because he has received him safe and sound, your father has killed the fatted calf.' 28 "But he was angry and would not go in. Therefore his father came out and pleaded with him. 29 "So he answered and said to [his] father, 'Lo, these many years I have been serving you; I never transgressed your commandment at any time; and yet you never gave me a young goat, that I might make merry with my friends. 30 'But as soon as this son of yours came, who has devoured your livelihood with harlots, you killed the fatted calf for him.' 31 "And he said to him, 'Son, you are always with me, and all that I have is yours. 32 'It was right that we should make merry and be glad, for your brother was dead and is alive again, and was lost and is found.' "

CHAPTER 14
MORE PERSIAN POETRY

A poem of Hafez:

مژده ای دل که مسیحا نفسی می آید   که ز انفاس خوشش بوی کسی می آید
ز غم هجر مکن ناله و فریاد که دوش   زده ام فالی و فریادرسی می آید
آتش وادی ایمن نه منم خرّم و بس   موسی آنجا به امید قبسی می آید
هیچ کس نیس که در کوی توآش کاری نیست   هر کس آنجا به طریق هوسی می آید
کس ندانست که منزلگه معشوق کجاست   این قدر هست که بانگ جرسی می آید
دوست را گر سر پرسیدن بیمار غم است   گو:"بر آن خوش که هنوزش نفسی می آید
خبر بلبل این باغ بپرسید که من   ناله ای می شنوم کز قفسی می آید
یار دارد سر آزردن حافظ یاران
شاهبازی به شکار مگسی می آید

O heart Glad tidings! A Christ-breath comes.
From whose fragrant breathings, one's fragrance comes.
Of grief of separation, make no complaint or plaint.
For, last night, I struck on omen; and a grievance-redresser comes.
Of Wadi Aymans fire, joyful, not only am I.
There, Moses in hope of a fire comes.
In thy street, is none who a great work has not.
There, in the way of a great desire, every one comes.
Where the Beloved's dwelling is, none knows.
This much is, that the clang of the bell comes.

If the desire of asking the health of one sick with grief be the Friends.
Say: "Go happily to him; for, yet, a breath of his comes."
Of the Nightingale of this garden, ask the news, For I Hear his lament that forth from the cage comes.
Friends! The true Beloved desires the prey of Hafiz's heart: For the prey of a little fly, a great falcon comes.

A poem of Ferdosi:

من این نامه شهریاران پیش   بگفتم بدین نغر گفتار خویش
همان نامداران و گردنکشان   که دادم یکایک از ایشان نشان
همه مرده از روزگار دراز   شد ازگفت من نامشان زنده باد
چو عیسی من از این مردگانرا تمام   سراسر همه زنده کردم بنام
بناهای آباد گردد خراب   زباران و از آتش آفتاب
پی افکندم از نظم کاخی بلند   که از باد و باران نیاید گزند

فردوسی

'These tales, which relate to the monarchs of old, In volumes of elegant verse I have told. The men of renown, and of prowess and fame, Whose' deeds are recorded herein name by name, Time swept them aside, and death stilled heart and brain,

But here in my verses they live once again. Like Jesus, whose voice called the dead back to life,

I've wakened dead heroes of struggle and strife. At long last each noble construction decays, Assaulted by wind and the sun's scorching rays. But I have erected a Palace of Rhyme: No blast shall o'erthrow it, nor passage of time.'

Another from Hafez:

گر روی پاک . مجرد چو مسیحا بفلک   از فروغ تو بخورشید رسد صد پرتو

حافظ

'If thou, like Christ, be pure and single-hearted,
Who once ascended far beyond the sky,
Thy life will shine with beams of light, whereby
The sun will brighten by thy light imparted.'

Another from Hafez:

فیض روح القدس ار باز مدد فرماید   دیگران هم بکنند آنچه مسیحا می کرد

حافظ

'And if the Holy Ghost descend
In grace and power infinite
His comfort in these days to lend
To them that humbly wait on it,
Theirs too the wondrous works can be
That Jesus wrought in Galilee,'

A poem of Hamdi Shirazi

یکی اقن.م از تثلیث اقدس	فروغ زندگی یعنی مسیحا
نهفته کبریای ذوالجلال	بهنجار بشر شد آشکارا
بدو بالاپران کردند شادی	ز شادی گشت گردون پر زغوغا
بهر سو مژده ها بردند و خواندند	بچوپانان میان دشت و صحرا
بفرمان خدا از دختر بکر	هویدا گشت نور شادی افزا
درخشان کوکبی از زادن او	بپام آسمان بر داشت آوا
چو ایرانی بدید آن اختر پاک	فراز چرخ چون خورشید عذرا

دوید آنجا که آنجا شاد و خندان   بدارد هدیه های خویش اهدا

حمیدی شیرازی

One Holy Person of the Trinity,
The Christ of God, the Light of Heaven and earth,
As man appeared among the sons of men;
Concealed his glory, majesty and worth.
The angels in the world above rejoiced;
The vault of heaven rang with joy and mirth.
To shepherds watching in the fields at night
They brought the tidings of his holy birth.
From a pure virgin by Divine command
Appeared the light that lighteneth man's days.
A brilliant star proclaimed the glad event:
In the far heaven shone its ardent blaze.
The Persian Magi saw, the effulgent star,
Illumining the sky like solar rays.
Towards Bethlehem with joyful steps they sped
To offer Him their precious gifts and praise.

CHAPTER 15
JESUS THE KING (THE MESSIAH)

Then came Jesus forth, wearing the crown of thorns, and the purple robe. And Pilate said unto them, "Behold the man!" (John 19:5, of the Bible)

Remember Jesus Christ ("the Anointed King"), risen from the dead, descendant of King David, according to my gospel... (2Timothy 2:8 of the Bible)

And when they could not find them, they dragged Jason and some of the brothers before the city authorities, shouting, "These men who have turned the world upside down have come here also, and Jason has received them, and they are all acting against the decrees of Caesar, saying that there is another king, Jesus." (Acts 17:6-7 of the Bible)

What Did Jesus Do?

Luke, a doctor and follower of King Jesus, wrote the book of the Bible known today as, "The Gospel of Luke." With the help of the Holy Spirit, he called it a record, "of all that Jesus began to do and teach" (Acts 1:1). Jesus did works, and he taught. When you consider a special person, a teacher or prophet, you must consider both their words and their life. What did King Jesus do? What did he teach?

Let's consider Jesus' life for now. The first amazing

thing about Jesus' life is that he *fulfilled prophecy*, prophecy previously given about him. This is not true of most prominent people, but it *characterizes* the Messiah[19], Jesus.

So, what is prophecy? It's a message, through people, that comes from God.[20] It's sometimes a prediction of the future, but not always. From near the beginning of the fall of mankind, God has communicated to humanity through prophets — special servants of his who he gifted to speak his words at times. It was through them that he wrote the Bible, over a period of over a thousand years. I will be quoting it throughout this book, starting with this:

...knowing this first of all, that no prophecy of Scripture comes from someone's own interpretation. For no prophecy was ever produced by the will of man, but men spoke from God as they were carried along by the Holy Spirit. (2Peter 1:20-21[21])

Predictions about Jesus, actually, first began in the Garden of Eden, before mankind was sent out of it. Let me stop and ask the question, "Why were they — the first man and woman — expelled from Paradise?" It was for more than eating an apple! This is what

---

[19] "Messiah" (from Hebrew) means **"the King/Priest Chosen and Empowered by God."** In Greek, the word is "Christos," where we get the term, "the Christ." The literal is, "the Anointed One"

[20] "God" (Hebrew: "EL") literally means, "the Powerful One." He's the One who created everything, who's all-knowing and all-powerful, pure love, completely right and good, and full of justice...we'll talk more about him

[21] Format means, "2nd Peter, chapter 1, verses 20 to 21."

happened: they were given everything—a perfect habitat, perfect bodies without pain or death, lives of adventure, relationship with God unlike any created beings on Earth, and the commission from God to rule on Earth as His representatives. Humans were created as royalty, as ambassadors of God's kingdom,[22] on Earth. They were commissioned to *subdue*, not the peaceful, created paradise but an army of rebellious fallen spirits. And God Himself would come down and spend periods of time with them. There was no division between original mankind and God. Their spiritual and physical senses were totally alive.

An amazing truth about God is that he, "tests the righteous."[23] He doesn't only test evil people. He tests the righteous. The first man and woman, who did everything right, who had everything, were tested. God told them they could eat of any tree of the Garden except one. They were given so much in the beginning, but they would soon lose it.

Eventually satan,[24] or "the devil,"[25] who was supposed to be subdued and dominated by the newly appointed representatives of God, approached the man and woman. This crafty being is called "the

---

[22] The political structure of God's country is a monarchy, a kingdom, of which He is the King

[23] Psalm 11:5, Jeremiah 20:12

[24] The name "satan" means, "the enemy" and "the resister." He resists God's purposes and people

[25] The "devil" literally means "through throwing." In other words, he's a coward and doesn't approach his targets directly. He attacks from a ways away and uses deception

serpent," as well as "the dragon."[26] It came in and LIED to the first people. Tragically, the first man and woman *listened to* and soon *believed* the enemy over God, and then they took the plunge...

The effect of this act can be seen in every aspect of life and society today.

How must have Adam and Eve felt, as they heard God approaching them in the Garden for a time of sharing and hanging out? They knew what they'd done was wrong and that the serpent had lied to them. They must have felt extremely dirty, unable to come into the light of God's face. The Bible says they hid themselves when he came near.

A "curse" simply means a judgment. God blesses and curses—he decrees good things for people and bad things. He is the Great Judge. And, in fact, someday he will judge all people, angels and evil spirits. During that dark day in the Garden of Eden, God had to pronounce a negative judgment on Adam and Eve, all their descendants, and even the physical creation.

Another amazing truth about God is that he's merciful. To those who have failed the tests in their life, his hand of mercy is open and extended. He's not spiteful, abusive, explosive, or vindictive. [27] God actually "delights in showing mercy."[28] So alongside the judgment that he gave, he also extended mercy.

---

[26] Revelation 20:2

[27] Those are actually characteristics of the enemy, who first uses deception to take people down and then attacks and accuses them for falling! God is the opposite

[28] Micah 7:18

When He pronounced judgment on the serpent also, he foretold of a way out of the pain and torment that was coming to humanity! He said to the devil:

I will put enmity between you and the woman, and between your offspring and her Offspring; he shall bruise your head, and you shall bruise his heel. (Genesis 3:15)

Consider this. After the fall, mankind lost its place of dominance. They're still like God in some ways but can't naturally know him, and can't represent him and subdue the rebel, satan or his army. But God spoke of a time when an Offspring of Eve would come. He would be bruised on his heel, while *bruising the serpent's head!* When King Jesus was crucified unjustly, he was bruising satan's head, he was crushing it under his foot. His heel was bruised in the process—and it was real pain, the worst of all. But he was removing satan's place of dominance over the human race, by removing humanity's guilt, for all who believe! ☺

For Christ also suffered once for sins, the righteous for the unrighteous, that he might bring us to God. (1Peter 3:18)

Virtually every detail of King Jesus' earthly life was documented beforehand, by ancient Hebrew prophets. He fulfilled the words of God, so that those in Israel with sincere hearts after God would recognize him when he came, by what he did. What did he do??? In one word: *miracles*.

With power from God, he healed sick people of

every kind of disease and evil spirit oppression. Some specific cases: he instantly cured a boy of leprosy. He healed a woman who for twelve years had a tormenting, bleeding problem. He healed a hunchback woman who'd been deformed for 18 years. He *raised a boy from the dead*, whose mother was a widow and had no one to care for her. He stopped a deadly storm on the sea. He removed evil spirits from an insane man, who could not be held by chains!

God's representative, Jesus, also forgave a woman who'd been in prostitution. Forgiveness is in itself a miracle. He forgave a paralyzed man of something he'd done and then healed him so he walked. He freed the tongues of many mute people and opened the ears of many deaf. He dealt with leprosy and all kinds of diseases. Imagine them: heart disease, lung problems, stomach cancer, teeth issues, foot problems, mental issues, and on and on. He was a Doctor — the best of them. These and many more of what Jesus did are recorded in Mathew, Mark, Luke, and John of the Bible.[29] And John stated at the end of his book:

Now there are also many other things that Jesus did. Were every one of them to be written, I suppose that the world itself could not contain the books that would be written. (John 22:25)

The greatest act that Jesus did, though, was not an obviously great one. It actually looked like a weak one. It wasn't raising someone from the dead, or healing anyone directly. It was that he became a sacrifice, a substitution for mankind. This was his

---

[29] The first four books of what's often called, "The New Testament"

greatest purpose in coming. All the people he healed eventually died. But he came to do something eternal. He came to deal with the root cause of every single problem that's ever been on Earth, and from there, to set a multitude of people from every nation free. How did he do this??

Therefore, just as sin came into the world through one man, and death through sin, and so death spread to all men because all sinned...as one trespass led to condemnation for all men, so one act of righteousness leads to justification[30] and life for all men. For as by the one man's disobedience the many were made sinners, so by the one man's obedience the many will be made righteous. (Romans 5:12, 18-19)

By obeying God's command to Jesus, to *selflessly* die for humanity, Jesus reversed the effect of Adam's *selfish* act. Just as real as the fact that all humans sin and all humans die, is the fact that Jesus' death can make you righteous and give you indestructible life. This is what God sent Jesus to do. He wants to *give* you righteousness.

When he hung on that execution instrument, the cross, all of God's judgment for all of each human's sins was poured out on him. Is it no wonder, at one point, in agony, Jesus had to cry out and ask his Father why?

About the ninth hour Jesus cried out with a loud voice, saying, "Eli, Eli, lema sabachthani?" that is,

---

[30] "Justification" means "making right" or "making righteous"

"My God, my God, why have you forsaken me? (Matthew 27:46)

We see from earlier writings of prophets that God answered this prayer of his. At that time, as Jesus hung naked and mutilated on the cross, fulfilling his destiny as the Lamb of God, the Father opened Jesus' eyes, and he saw the future. What do you think he saw? He saw, "his offspring,"[31] those who his great work would make righteous, those who would believe in him and be saved by him. He saw you! Then it says, "he was satisfied."

Someone had to pay for the sins. You could do it. But God *is love*,[32] and his love for *you* was too great to not give you a solution.

For God so loved the world, that he gave his only Son, that whoever believes in him should not perish ["die"] but have eternal life. For God did not send his Son into the world to condemn the world, but in order that the world might be saved through him...Whoever believes in the Son has eternal life; whoever does not obey the Son shall not see life, but the wrath of God remains on him. (John 3:16-17, 36)

What is "the wrath of God"? Wrath means *fierce anger*. God is pure and holy, beyond what any of us can imagine. That purity is in 180-degree opposition to evil. There's no evil in God, and none will be allowed to remain in His universe. Evil and those

---

[31] Isaiah 53:10-11, Hebrews 12:2

[32] 1John 4:16

who live in it are doomed to be destroyed. But at this time, though the ship is going down, God has offered lifeboats to *ALL* humanity. He poured his wrath out on His Son, King Jesus. We can now escape the judgment of "perishing" eternally, through Jesus.

This Messiah, this King was different than any other. He didn't lift himself up; he came on a mission to die — for you and me. As he said about Himself,

The Son of Man[33] came not to be served but to serve, and to give his life as a ransom for many. (Mark 10:43)

When he died a brutal death penalty, which he did not deserve, he was taking the role of a lamb sacrifice, a substitute, *for fallen humanity*. He is the slain lamb.[34] As such, he is "the satisfying sacrifice for our sins."[35] In other words, he took the judgment due to Adam, Eve, and all humanity that followed, so that God sees the sacrifice and is fully satisfied. JESUS PAID THE PRICE FOR ALL HUMAN EVIL. God can lift the ban on humanity and give us full forgiveness, reunion with him, and eternal life.

Three days after his death, after he paid the full penalty for all of humanity's sins, King Jesus rose again. He's alive; the Father raised him from the dead and lifted him to the highest throne, his rightful place

---

[33] This is one of the titles of Jesus, which he often used about himself. "Man" is the same word in the original language as, "Adam." Jesus came as a descendent of Adam, in order to save the human or "adamic" race

[34] Revelation 13:8, John 1:29-36

[35] 1John 2:2

at the Father's side. He has supreme authority in Heaven and on Earth, as God's appointed King. At this time, he is not fully exerting his authority on Earth, because now is the temporary time period in which all have the right to receive him by faith and be saved.

Do you see him? Do you see his mercy, how he stepped out of heaven for you, to take your place in the death sentence? Do you see that God, according to his promises spoken through his prophets, raised him from the dead? If you believe in this in your heart, it's because God has revealed it to you. He wants a relationship with you. He sent his Son for you to bring you back to him. His door is open WIDE to you. Enter in and know God. Receive the gift he has freely given.

How do you receive this gift? You have to bow your knee in full submission to the risen King, Jesus, acknowledging him as Lord. [36] This kind of commitment is not cheap; nor can it be forced on you by anybody. It's got to be a genuine act, from the heart. When you allow Jesus — the highest King — into your life, he comes in as the KING. You submit to him, and the GREAT BENEFIT of having him in your life, is that he *saves* you. The mercy of the cross is applied to your life, *forever*.

I urge you to chose God, your Creator, the only one who can give you eternal life and so many *wonderful, indescribable* things in this life. Though the path will not be easy, God will give you supernatural peace, joy, many gifts, knowledge of him, wisdom, mental and physical healing, and so much more. But the

---

[36] "Lord" means "Authority"

entrance into this life is like a narrow gate. You've gotta make the full-on TRUST choice, to let go of your life and hand it over to God, it's rightful owner.

Bow to the King, Jesus, and submit full allegiance to Him. Then he will save you, as you call out to him. He will forgive you of *ALL* past sins—He alone can do that. He will cleanse your conscience and give you a new heart.

If you acknowledge with your mouth that Jesus is Lord [making him YOUR Lord—your highest Authority] and believe in your heart that God raised him from the dead, you *will be saved*. For with the heart one believes and is justified [made righteous], and with the mouth one verbally acknowledges and is saved. For the Scripture says, "Everyone who believes in him will not be put to shame." For there is no distinction between Jew and Greek [or any other people]; for the same Lord is Lord of all, bestowing his riches on all who call on him. For "everyone who calls on the name of the Lord will be saved." (Romans 10:9-13)

Don't wait.

The act that Jesus commands you to do, along with calling on Him to save you, is baptism, that is, that you be immersed[37] in water.

After Jesus rose from the dead, he appeared to hundreds of his disciples[38] for a period of forty days, and he said these things to them:

---

[37] "Baptism" literally means "immersion"

[38] "Disciple" means "Student" or "Apprentice"

All authority in heaven and on earth has been given to me. Go therefore and make disciples of all nations, baptizing them [i.e., immersing them in water]. [Do this] in the name[39] of the Father and of the Son and of the Holy Spirit, teaching them to observe all that I have commanded you. And behold, I am with you every day, to the end of the age. (Matthew 28:18-20)

And he said to them, "Go into all the world and proclaim the gospel [40] to the whole creation. Whoever believes and is baptized will be saved, but whoever does not believe will be condemned. And these signs will accompany those who believe: in my name they will cast out demons[41]; they will speak in new tongues[42]; they will pick up serpents with their hands; and if they drink any deadly poison, it will not hurt them; they will lay their hands on the sick, and they will recover." So then the Lord Jesus, after he had spoken to them, was taken up into heaven and sat down at the right hand of God. And they went out and preached everywhere, while the Lord worked with them and confirmed the message by accompanying [supernatural] signs. (Mark 16:15-20)

The last work Jesus did while on Earth was to send

---

[39] In other words, in the authority of"

[40] "Gospel" means, "Good News"

[41] "Demons" means evil spirits

[42] Languages (a supernatural gift for all who believe)

his Students out into all the world, with the mission of telling "the Gospel," the good news about Jesus — who He is, what he did for the world on the cross, and what he will do for them personally if they accept him as King. He also gave them a promise: he would be with them as they went and he would back the message up with miraculous signs. This promise is true today. As one of Jesus' Students, I am telling you God's message. He wants you to be close to him, so much so he sacrificed his Son Jesus, so you can live and know him. He WILL forgive your sins — no matter how great. He can do it because Jesus took your death penalty already. That's how much love he has for you. He wants to accept you and save you from death and judgment.

If you are sick or have pain right now, place your hand on the problem area and hear these words, which I speak for you: "Jesus, I know you love this person, and you want them to be yours. In the authority of Jesus, I command the pain, sickness, and disability of the person's body: be healed! Now! Spirit of affliction and sickness, leave this person. Go now!"

How Jesus Deals With the *ROOTS*

It's wonderful, GOOD NEWS that God deals with the roots of our problems. What we would overlook and not even address, he sees clearly and decided to provide a Solution for. Consider this conversation King Jesus had with a political and religious leader in Israel:

Now there was a man of the Pharisees[43] **named Nicodemus, a ruler of the Jews.**[44] **This man came to Jesus by night**[45] **and said to him, "Rabbi, we know that you are a teacher come from God, for no one can do these signs that you do unless God is with him." Jesus answered him, "Truly, truly, I say to you, unless one is born again he cannot see the kingdom**[46] **of God. (John 3:1-3)**

With this statement, Jesus brought out a truth that is invaluable: without a new birth, the human race can never even see God's kingdom.

Nicodemus said to him, "How can a man be born when he is old? Can he enter a second time into his mother's womb and be born?" (John 3:4)

---

[43] A religious group of that day; they were very devout, but most of them missed the promised Messiah, and gave him over to be crucified. Their religion wasn't enough; they needed a Savior

[44] The Book of John was written partly to Gentiles (non-Jews), so often the term "the Jews" is used, since Jesus only worked in Israel while on Earth. "Jews," in the Book of John, sometimes refers to people from the province of Judea, which included Jerusalem (see John 11:7-8). Sometimes it refers to all "Hebrews," as the term is used today, those descended from Abraham, Isaac, and Jacob (see John 4:22). In this sense, Jesus is a Jew, as is John, the writer of this book, though they were not from Judea but Galilee, another province in Israel

[45] He came by night because of fear. The whole atmosphere of Judea at that time was tense because of threats from the political & religious leaders. They envied, and hated Jesus, because of his teaching and miracles, and used fear to keep people from following him (see John 9:22, 12:42)

[46] The "kingdom of God" means God's domain, his territory or country, his reign, and his government

Man cannot know what he is without revelation from God. At man's creation, God formed man's body of the dust of the Earth, but he had no life until God breathed into his nostrils. Then man became a living being.[47] The life that entered man's body was the human spirit. Man was now living in his earthly body, with a mind and emotions. The term "soul" in the Bible often refers to a person's mind and emotions.[48]

The first woman was made after man had been created. She was actually taken out of the man.[49] Both of them, then, had a spirit, a soul, and a body. These three elements make up what a human being is.[50]

It is so important to understand this next valuable truth:

God created man in his own image, in the image of God he created him; male and female he created him. (Genesis 1:27)

When God created man, he did so very, *very* differently than the way he created animals. He used his creativity to make a huge diversity of living beings, but when it came to mankind, he used his own image to create them.

Notice also that it's the combination of a male and

---

[47] Genesis 2:7

[48] "Soul" also sometimes also means, "being," and sometimes, "self-centered will," depending on context

[49] Genesis 2:18-25

[50] 1Thessalonians 5:23

female which is the complete image of God. God encompasses both.

Now let's come to why Jesus taught that mankind must be reborn. In the Garden, after creating man and woman, God considered his creation "very good."[51] By looking at the world today, we see that it is not "very good" anymore, and we understand that there was a fall.

The Lord God commanded the man, saying, "You may surely eat of every tree of the garden, but of the tree of the knowledge of good and evil you shall not eat, for in the day that you eat of it you shall surely die. (Genesis 2:16-17)

What part of man and woman died on the day they ate the forbidden fruit? It was not their minds — they kept on thinking and living once expelled from the Garden. Their bodies kept on living as well for a while. It was their spirit, the essence of who they were, the connection they had to God and to the spiritual realms.

It's hard for us to understand death outside of the physical realm. What does it mean that their spirit died? At least part of the answer is that it was cut off from God. It lost connection to God, the source of its life and light. Afterward, as Adam and Eve reproduced, all their children were born with the same lack of connection to God. All humanity was born dead spiritually, but Jesus, though born as a man, was born alive.[52]

---

[51] Genesis 1:31

[52] Through what's been called, "the immaculate conception." See Luke 1:31-37

When Jesus was sent to solve the problems of mankind, his job started at the roots—saving man's spirit.

Jesus answered, "Truly, truly, I say to you, unless one is born of water and the Spirit, he cannot enter the kingdom of God. That which is born of the flesh is flesh, and that which is born of the Spirit is spirit. Do not marvel that I said to you, 'You must be born again.' The wind blows where it wishes, and you hear its sound, but you do not know where it comes from or where it goes. So it is with everyone who is born of the Spirit. (John 3:5-8)

The "born of water" part relates to being, "born of the flesh." Your mother's water broke while you were in the womb, and you were born out of her body. This birth refers to our physical bodies. To be "born again" means to be "born of the Spirit." This Spirit is the "Spirit of God," introduced in the very beginning of Genesis. He's part of God.

Jesus came to bring *life* to the earth, a kind of life that was lost by mankind. At one point, Jesus was speaking with a crowd of people:

Jesus then said to them, "Truly, truly, I say to you, it was not Moses who gave you the bread from heaven,[53] but my Father gives you the true bread

---

[53] God used Moses to lead his People—the descendants of Abraham, Isaac, and Jacob—out of slavery in Egypt. He led them into the desert, on the way to a land he'd promised to give them. In the desert, he provided for them supernaturally, including their food. However, that food was only a shadow of the true bread from Heaven, Jesus

from heaven. For the bread of God is he who comes down from heaven and gives life to the world." They said to him, "Sir, give us this bread always." Jesus said to them, "I am the bread of life; whoever comes to me will not hunger, and whoever believes in me will never thirst. But I said to you that you have seen me and yet do not believe. All that the Father gives me will come to me, and whoever comes to me I will never cast out. For I have come down from heaven, not to do my own will but the will of him who sent me. And this is the will of him who sent me, that I should lose nothing of all that he has given me, but raise it up on the last day. For this is the will of my Father, that everyone who looks on the Son and believes in him should have eternal life, and I will raise him up on the last day."

So the Jews grumbled about him, because he said, "I am the bread that came down from heaven." They said, "Is not this Jesus, the son of Joseph, whose father and mother we know? How does he now say, 'I have come down from heaven'?" Jesus answered them, "Do not grumble among yourselves. No one can come to me unless the Father who sent me draws him. And I will raise him up on the last day. It is written in the Prophets, 'And they will all be taught by God.' Everyone who has heard and learned from the Father comes to me—not that anyone has seen the Father except he who is from God; he has seen the Father.

Truly, truly, I say to you, whoever believes has eternal life. I am the bread of life. Your fathers ate the manna in the wilderness, and they died. This is the bread that comes down from heaven, so that one may eat of it and not die. I am the living bread that came down from heaven. If anyone eats of this bread, he will live forever. And the bread that I will give for the life of the world is my flesh. The Judeans then disputed among themselves, saying, "How can this man give us his flesh to eat?" So Jesus said to them, "Truly, truly, I say to you, unless you eat the flesh of the Son of Man and drink his blood, you have no life in you. Whoever feeds on my flesh and drinks my blood has eternal life, and I will raise him up on the last day. For my flesh is true food, and my blood is true drink. Whoever feeds on my flesh and drinks my blood abides in me, and I in him. As the living Father sent me, and I live because of the Father, so whoever feeds on me, he also will live because of me. (John 6:32-57)

Do you want to live? If this is making sense to you at all, God is inviting you to his Son Jesus, so you can receive life. You will receive spiritual life; you will be born again. And this life goes on forever.

Immersion in Water

When Jesus rose from the dead, he interacted with his Students of that time for forty days. At the end of this time, the King gave his Students a commission, which included these words.

He said to them, "Go into all the world and proclaim the gospel to the whole creation. Whoever believes and is baptized will be saved, but whoever does not believe will be condemned.... (Mark 16:15-

16)

Shortly after King Jesus commissioned his Students and ascended, Peter spoke to a large crowd in Jerusalem, where Jesus had just been crucified. The crowd was astonished to realize that they'd missed God's chosen Messiah for them, and let him be crucified!!! They were cut to the heart as they believed the truth they heard. Peter shouted out at the end of his message:

"...Let all the house of Israel therefore know for certain that God has made him both Lord and Christ, this Jesus whom you crucified." Now when they heard this they were cut to the heart, and said to Peter and the rest of the apostles, "Brothers, what shall we do?" And Peter said to them, "Repent and be baptized every one of you in the name of Jesus Christ for the forgiveness of your sins, and you will receive the gift of the Holy Spirit. 39 The promise is for you and your children and for all who are far off—for all whom the Lord our God will call." 40 With many other words he warned them; and he pleaded with them, "Save yourselves from this corrupt generation." 41 Those who accepted his message were baptized, and about three thousand were added to their number that day. (Acts 2:36-41)

They'd made a big, BIG mistake. But God is merciful. He provided a Solution to their dilemma—Jesus' death, the very thing they were partially guilty of! God is a merciful forgiver of sins. He was willing to forgive and save them. The fact that they just helped crucify His Son did not stop him, because He

IS love, and he is able to forgive.

In verse 38, above, Peter told them how to respond to the Good News: repent and be immersed in water. To "repent" means to *change*. It's a change of heart that will result in a change of life. These people had been against their Messiah, Jesus, but it was now time for them to change, to make him their Lord, to call on him to save them. Their WHOLE LIFE would be affected totally by this change. The same is true for you, friend.

In Jesus commission, another thing he said was,

"Thus it is written, that the Christ should suffer and on the third day rise from the dead, and that repentance and forgiveness of sins should be proclaimed in his name to all nations, beginning from Jerusalem" (Luke 24:46-47)

Notice that changing the way you think ("repentance") comes *before* forgiveness of sins. If a person doesn't truly bow to the Authority, Jesus, from the heart, in light of the Message, that person cannot obtain forgiveness. Forgiveness is in the authority of the King, Jesus, and in His authority alone, as God sent *HIM* as the savior. You try to get God's forgiveness any other way, and He won't give it to you.

This Jesus is the stone that was rejected by you[54], the builders, which has become the cornerstone.

---

[54] The Student, Peter, was speaking to his fellow Jews in Jerusalem in this verse, who had shortly before rejected their Messiah, having not recognized his humble form

And there is salvation in no one else, for there is no other name[55] under heaven given among men by which we must be saved. (Acts 4:11-12)

Maybe you've even heard of Jesus and even agreed that he rose from the dead, but haven't personally submitted to him as Lord, directly. Now is the time.

On one occasion, Jesus used a man named Ananias to heal someone who had been struck blind. The healed man recounted what happened to him in Scripture:

12 "A man named Ananias came to see me. He was a devout observer of the law[56] and highly respected by all the Jews living there. 13 He stood beside me and said, 'Brother Saul, receive your sight!' And at that very moment I was able to see him. 14 "Then he said: 'The God of our ancestors has chosen you to know his will and to see the Righteous One and to hear words from his mouth. 15 You will be his witness to all people of what you have seen and heard. 16 *And now what are you waiting for? Get up, be baptized and wash your sins away, calling on his name.*' (Acts 22:12-16)

Your next and immediate step is to be baptized — immersed in water.

Find a Student of Jesus, a sincere follower of Jesus, and ask them to immerse you in water. You can use

---

[55] Or, "authority"

[56] The Law of Moses, given to the Jews before Christ came. He was also a follower of King Jesus

any body of water—a river, lake, swimming pool, a bathtub, etc. You don't need a religious leader to do it, just a Student of Jesus. Because of religious tradition, the person may hesitate, try to postpone it, or try to get a religious leader to do it—if so, demand they do it right away or find someone else to do it.[57]

Recognize that this is a commitment you are making before God, pledging yourself to Him. You're not being immersed into *any* human organization or "church," but into "the name (or "authority") of Jesus."[58] You connect with God and His Kingdom as you're immersed.

One woman I know of made Jesus her Lord in a dangerously oppressive country. She could not find anyone to baptize her, including the Christians she new, so she had to baptize herself in the Name of the Lord Jesus.[59] Though typically a Student of Jesus is to immerse a new Student, this woman did the right thing in obedience to her new King. It changed her life.

Again, it's immersion "in the name of Jesus," meaning it's a spiritual thing that is covered by His authority. So it will have a powerful effect on your life. As you do it you are to commit yourself to God.[60]

---

[57] Religious tradition passed down through the centuries always distorts, diminishes, and delays immersion in water for new believers, but the Bible shows new converts *always* being immersed immediately after choosing Jesus, according to Jesus' command

[58] Acts 2:38, 10:48

[59] Her story is in her book, "I Dared to Call Him Father."

[60] 1Peter 3:21

The analogy of the water is that your sins, which have been forgiven, are being washed away.

For a new believer, immersion is totally urgent.[61] Be immersed in water right away, without delay.

After you've been immersed in water, you can freely download a PDF version the full book, "Jesus the King - with First Steps", at

www.actschristianity.com

It includes a section called, "First Steps," to help you grow on Jesus' narrow path to Life.

For the Gospel in Farsi:

www.hayateabadi.org

My testimony is also shared online:

https://youtu.be/Gk68mege8II

---

[61] Acts 16:33, Acts 2216, Acts 10:48, Acts 8:35-38

www.ingramcontent.com/pod-product-compliance
Lightning Source LLC
Chambersburg PA
CBHW061942070426
42450CB00007BA/1026